CALL to CELEBRATE
RECONCILIATION & EUCHARIST

This book belongs to

Niya Butler

Harcourt Religion Publishers

Author
Maureen A. Kelly, M.A.

Nihil Obstat
Msgr. Louis R. Piermarini
Imprimatur
✢Most Rev. Robert J. McManus, S.T.D.
Bishop of Worcester
February 2, 2006

The Imprimatur is an official declaration that a book or pamphlet is free of doctrinal or moral error. No implication is contained therein that anyone who granted the Imprimatur agrees with the contents, opinions, or statements expressed.

Text Credits

For permission to reprint copyrighted material, grateful acknowledgment is made to the following sources:

Michael Balhoff: Lyrics from "Remember Your Love" by Mike Balhoff. Lyrics © 1973, 1978 by Damean Music. Lyrics from "We Praise You" by Mike Balhoff, Darryl Ducote, and Gary Daigle. Lyrics © 1978 by Damean Music.

John Burland: Lyrics from "Come to the Table" by John Burland. Lyrics copyright © 2005 by John Burland. Lyrics from "Coming Back Together" by John Burland. Lyrics copyright © 2000 by John Burland. Lyrics from "Yes Lord, I Believe!" by John Burland. Lyrics © 2000 by John Burland.

Division of Christian Education of the National Council of the Churches of Christ in the U.S.A.: Scripture quotations from the *New Revised Standard Version Bible Catholic Edition.* Text copyright © 1993 and 1989 by the Division of Christian Education of the National Council of the Churches of Christ in the U.S.A

GIA Publications, Inc., 7404 S. Mason Ave., Chicago, IL 60638 www.giamusic.com 800-442-1358: Lyrics from "I Will Praise You, Lord" by Tony Alonso. Lyrics © 2003 by GIA Publications, Inc. Lyrics from "We Are Called" by David Haas. Lyrics copyright 1988 by GIA Publications, Inc.

International Commission on English in the Liturgy: From the English translation of "Blessing After Meals" in Book of Blessings. Translation © 1988 by International Committee on English in the Liturgy, Inc. From the English translation of the *Rite of Christian Initiation of Adults.* Translation © 1985 by International Committee on English in the Liturgy, Inc. From the English translation of *The Roman Missal.* Translation © 1973 by International Committee on English in the Liturgy, Inc. From the English translation of "Come, Holy Spirit" in *A Book of Prayers.* Translation © 1982 by International Committee on English in the Liturgy, Inc. From the English translation of *Rite of Penance.* Translation © 1974 by International Committee on English in the Liturgy, Inc. From the English translation of Psalm Refrains in *Lectionary for Mass.* Translation © 1969, 1981, 1997 by International Committee on English in the Liturgy, Inc.

International Consultation on English Texts: English translation of Hail Mary, Gloria in Excelsis, and the Apostles' Creed by the International Consultation on English Texts (ICET).

OCP Publications, 5536 NE Hassalo, Portland, OR 97213: Lyrics from "Show Us Your Mercy, O Lord/Misericordia, Señor" by Bob Hurd. English lyrics copyright © 1998 by Bob Hurd; Spanish lyrics © by Sobicain. Lyrics from "Lead Us to the Water" by Tom Kendzia, Gary Daigle, and John Foley. Lyrics © 1998 by Tom Kendzia, Gary Daigle and John Foley. Lyrics from "Open My Eyes" by Jesse Manibusan. Lyrics © 1988 by Jesse Manibusan. Published by spiritandsong.com®. Lyrics from "Children of God" by Christopher Walker. Lyrics © 1991 by Christopher Walker.

Illustration Credits

Dan Brown/Artworks 122–123, Shane Marsh/Linden Artists, Ltd. 62–63, 92–93, 142–143; Roger Payne/Linden Artists, Ltd. 42–43, 52–53, 112–113; Francis Phillips/Linden Artists, Ltd. 22–23, 32–33, 162–163; Tracy Somers 36, 56, 96, 97, 107, 146, 166, 167; Clive Spong/Linden Artists, Ltd. 12–13, 102–103, 132–133, 152–153.

Photo Credits

Laurent Emmanuel/Corbis Sygma 104; Royalty-Free/Corbis 20.

Printed in the United States of America

ISBN: 0-15-901653-3

2 3 4 5 6 7 8 9 10 030 10 09 08 07

Contents

Dear Candidate,

This is a very special time for you. You are preparing to take another step in your journey of friendship with Jesus and the Church. Your journey began when you were baptized. This journey of faith never ends. You will keep growing in your friendship with Jesus and the Church for your whole life.

Sometimes on our journey with Jesus we act in ways that hurt our friendship with him. We are sorry and want to be forgiven. We want to change and grow even closer to him. The Church gives us the Sacrament of Reconciliation to help us know that God forgives us and brings us back to him.

You are getting ready to celebrate the Sacrament of Reconciliation for the first time. In this sacrament, Jesus forgives your sins through the actions and prayers of the priest.

In *Call to Celebrate: Reconciliation*, you will

- learn that God is a God of mercy and forgiveness
- pray with your classmates and family
- listen to the stories of Jesus and the Apostles
- learn how to celebrate the Sacrament of Reconciliation

What is one thing you would like to learn this year?

I want to leann about Jesus and how to use the Bible.

1 We Are Called

CELEBRATE

We Gather

Procession

As you sing, walk forward slowly. Follow the person carrying the Bible.

🎼 *Sing together.*

We are called to act with justice,
We are called to love tenderly,
We are called to serve one
    another,
to walk humbly with God.

David Haas © 1998 GIA Publications

We Listen

Leader: Let us pray.

Make the Sign of the Cross together.

Leader: A reading from the Acts of the Apostles.

Read Acts 17:22–34.
The word of the Lord.

All: Thanks be to God.

Sit silently.

Ritual Focus: Signing with the Cross

Leader: Let us call to mind the goodness of God who gives us all good things. God gives us life and breath, and in him we live and move and have our being.

Come to the water to be marked with the Sign of the Cross.

[Name], God calls you by name to live in love with him always.

Candidate: Amen.

We Go Forth

Leader: Let us join in the prayer that Jesus taught us:

Pray the Lord's Prayer together.

Leader: Loving God, our source of life, bless us, protect us from all evil, and bring us to everlasting life.

All: Amen.

🎵 *Sing the opening song together.*

God Calls

SIGNS OF FAITH

Baptismal Name

We are each given a special name at **Baptism**. Usually it is the name or some form of the name of a saint or Mary, the Mother of Jesus. It may be the name of an Old Testament person. The name given at Baptism does not have to be a saint's name. Sometimes the word for a virtue, such as Faith, Hope, or Charity, is used as a name.

Reflect

Signing with the cross Think about the celebration, and in the space provided, write responses to two of the following questions.

1. What did the celebration tell you about God?

2. What did you think was the most important part of the celebration for you? Why?

3. What does it mean to be signed with the Sign of the Cross?

4. How did you feel when you heard the words, "God calls you by name"?

Question 1

_____

_____

_____

_____

Question 4

_____

_____

_____

God's Children

At our Baptism the priest or deacon calls us by name. The whole community welcomes us with great joy. We are baptized in the name of God the Father, God the Son, and God the Holy Spirit. The priest or deacon makes the Sign of the Cross on our forehead. The Sign of the Cross is a sign we belong to God. It marks us as a Christian, a follower or disciple of Jesus.

God calls us to a life of happiness with him. He promises us his grace. **Grace** is a sharing in God's own life. Imagine that! God wants us to share his life; he wants us to be his children. He chooses us to love him and each other.

SIGNS OF FAITH

Baptism

Baptism is the sacrament that makes us children of God and members of the Body of Christ, the Church. Baptism takes away original sin and all personal **sin**. It unites us to Jesus and it makes us temples of the Holy Spirit. It promises us eternal life in heaven. In Baptism we celebrate God's promise that he will live in friendship with us forever.

God Loves Us

Faith Focus

How does God show his love for us?

God called Paul to tell people about Jesus and his message of good news. Paul answered God's call and traveled to many places to preach to people who had never heard of Jesus or his message. They worshiped false gods and built altars and temples to them. In the city of Athens, Paul was frustrated when he saw so many idols. So he stood up in the marketplace and spoke these words:

Scripture

ACTS 17:22–34

God Gives Everyone Life

"People of Athens! I see that in every respect you are very religious. For as I walked around looking carefully at your shrines, I even discovered an altar inscribed 'To an Unknown God.' I want to tell you about the unknown God. The God who made the world and all that is in it, the Lord of heaven and earth, does not dwell in shrines made by human hands. He does not need human hands. It is he who made the world and all that is in it. He is the Lord of heaven and earth. He gives everyone life and breath. He made everything, the sun and moon and stars, the seasons of the year.

"He wants people to search for him because he is not far from any one of us. For, 'In him we live and move and have our being.' We are his offspring, his children. Since we are his offspring, we should not think of God as an image fashioned from gold or silver or stone by human art or imagination. Until now God overlooked your ignorance, but now he demands that all people everywhere repent and believe in him."

Some of the Greeks believed what Paul told them and became followers of Jesus.

BASED ON ACTS 17:22–34

? **What does Paul teach the people of Athens about God?**

? **How do you answer God's call to search for him?**

Faith at Home

Read the scripture story with your family members. Discuss the different ways you and your family have come to know God. Examples could be through other people, events, and prayer. Make a list of those ways and use it by yourself or with family members as a litany of thanksgiving at mealtimes or other times when you are together. Read each item and respond, "We give you thanks, good and gracious God."

Share

Make a list With a partner or in small groups, make a list of words that you can share with other young people that would tell them where they can search for God.

Signs of God's Love

SIGNS OF FAITH

The Holy Trinity

God the Father, God the Son, and God the Holy Spirit are the three Persons in one God. We call them the **Holy Trinity**. Each of them can be called God. Belief in the Trinity is the most important part of our faith. When we make the Sign of the Cross, we are saying we believe in the Trinity.

Faith Focus

What are the sacraments?

From the very beginning, God wanted people to be friends with him. He shared his life with humans. But the first humans turned away from God's friendship. They disobeyed him and sinned. We call this first sin **original sin**. Original sin affects all people. Because of it, suffering came into the world and people tend to sin.

Even after the first humans turned away from him, God still wanted to live in friendship with people. So, God our Father sent his Son, Jesus, to show us how much he loves us. Jesus is the most important sign of God's love.

- Jesus showed us how to live in friendship with God.

- Jesus died on the cross to save us from sin.

- Jesus showed us that even when we turn from God's friendship, God will forgive us.

The Sacraments of Initiation

Jesus gave us the sacraments, so we would know God's love, forgiveness, healing, and call to service. A **sacrament** is an effective sign that comes from Jesus. The seven sacraments give us grace.

Baptism is the first of the three **Sacraments of Initiation**. In Baptism we are united to Jesus and receive new life. In **Confirmation** the Holy Spirit gives us strength to live as followers of Jesus. Baptism and Confirmation mark us with a special character, so we can only receive them once.

In the **Eucharist** we receive the Body and Blood of Jesus. We can participate in the Eucharist often. The Eucharist helps us be more like Jesus. It helps us live and move and have our being in God. We need to celebrate Reconciliation before First Eucharist.

These three sacraments together make us full members of the Church. The Church is a sign of God's love. God calls us to live in community with other people who believe in him. The Church family helps us grow as God's children.

? **What are some signs of God's love in your life?**

Faith at Home

Discuss the question and your family members' responses together. Ask others to share how Jesus is God's greatest sign of love for them. Ask family members to tell one of their favorite stories of Jesus from the Gospels and tell what qualities of Jesus they see in the story.

15

Being a Member

Respond

Build a church   With a partner or small group, talk about what it means to be a member of the Church. Then, in each of the building blocks below, write one thing that members of the Church do to show they are active members. Choose one of the actions that you are able to do and do it this week.

Usher Members

Help With the Eucharist

members

Closing Blessing

Gather and begin with the Sign of the Cross.

Leader: God, our Father, you give us all the living creatures.

All: We praise and thank you.

Leader: Jesus, our Savior, you give us life.

All: We praise and thank you.

Leader: Holy Spirit, our Helper, you make us holy.

All: We praise and thank you.

Leader: Let us go forth in peace and love.

All: Thanks be to God.

🎼 *Sing together.*

We are called to act with justice,
We are called to love tenderly,
We are called to serve one another,
to walk humbly with God.

David Haas © 1998 GIA Publications

Faith at Home

Faith Focus

- In Baptism God calls us to a life of happiness with him.

- A sacrament is an effective sign that comes from Jesus and gives us grace.

- Jesus is the greatest sign of God the Father's love.

Ritual Focus
Signing with the Cross

The celebration focused on being signed with holy water. You came to the water, were called by name, and signed with the Sign of the Cross. During the week, sign yourself with the Sign of the Cross when you wake up and remember that you belong to God.

Family Prayer

God, our Father, thank you for calling us to be your children. We know your love, and we want to share it with others. Send your Holy Spirit to help us love and care for everything you have created. We ask this in the name of your Son, Jesus. Amen.

Act

Share Together Read Isaiah 43:1–4. Invite family members to share how the reading makes them feel. Then talk together about the phrase, "I have called you by name, you are mine." Invite family members to share why they have the names they do. Then ask individuals to share what they like about their names. Have everyone be still and imagine God saying each of their names and adding, "You are mine."

Do Together God calls us to live in harmony with nature and to enjoy it. With your family, choose one of the following to do as a family this week:

- Go on a nature walk.
- Discuss how your family can be stewards of water.
- Find an environmental project to become involved in.
- Volunteer to help take care of an elderly neighbor's yard.

 www.harcourtreligion.com
Visit our Web site for weekly scripture readings and questions, family resources, and more activities.

2 We Are Welcomed

We Gather

Procession

As you sing, walk forward slowly. Follow the person carrying the Bible.

♪ *Sing together.*

We are marching in the light
  of God,
We are marching in the light
  of God,
We are marching, we are
  marching in the light of God.
We are marching, we are
  marching in the light of God.

South African Traditional

Leader: Let us pray.

Make the Sign of the Cross together.

Ritual Focus: Renewal of Baptismal Promises

Leader: Jesus is the Light of the World.

Light the candle.

Let us renew our baptismal promises now.

Do you reject sin so as to live in the freedom of God's children?

All: I do.

Leader: Do you reject Satan, and all his works, and all his empty promises?

All: I do.

Leader: Do you believe in God, the Father almighty; in Jesus Christ, his only Son, our Lord; in the Holy Spirit and the holy catholic Church?

All: I do.

BASED ON RITE OF BAPTISM FOR CHILDREN, 145–146

Sprinkle young people with water.

Make the Sign of the Cross as you are sprinkled with water.

We Listen

Leader: Good and gracious Father, send us the Holy Spirit to open our hearts to the good news of your Son, Jesus, the Light of the World. We ask this in his name.

All: Amen.

Leader: A reading from the holy Gospel according to Luke.

All: Glory to you, Lord.

Leader: *Read Luke 19:1–10.*

The Gospel of the Lord.

All: Praise to you, Lord Jesus Christ.

Sit silently.

We Go Forth

Leader: Loving Father, thank you for the Light of Christ. Send us the Holy Spirit to help us live as children of the light.

All: Amen.

♪ *Sing the opening song together.*

The Light of Christ

SIGNS OF FAITH

Holy Water

Water blessed by a **priest** for a religious purpose is called **holy water**. We use holy water to make the Sign of the Cross and to remember our Baptism.

Reflect

Renewal of Baptismal Promises   During the celebration you renewed your baptismal promises and were sprinkled with holy water. Think about the next week, and write a paragraph about how you will keep your baptismal promises throughout the week.

_____

_____

_____

_____

_____

_____

_____

_____

_____

Children of the Light

At Baptism we receive a candle. The priest prays that we will walk as children of the light. We are children of the light when we make choices to grow in our friendship with Jesus and the Church, and to love and care about other people.

Sometimes we do not act like children of the light. Even though we love our family or friends, we may choose to do things that are unloving. Even though we feel sorry for people who are poor or in need, we do not reach out to them. Sometimes we choose not to care about or share what we have with them. When we do that, we choose sin.

We know what it is like to choose to do something wrong. We know what it is like to feel sorry and want to make up. What if we never got a second chance?

SIGNS OF FAITH

Candles

Candles are signs of Christ, the Light of the World. Candles are used at the altar during Mass. The most important candle used in the sacraments is the **Paschal candle**. This candle is blessed at the Easter Vigil and burned during the Masses of the Easter season. It is also burned at Baptisms and funerals throughout the year. Sometimes candles are placed before the altars of Mary and the saints. These candles are a sign of respect and prayer.

Jesus Brings Good News

Faith Focus

What happens when Jesus welcomes us?

Jesus welcomed sinners. He ate and drank with them. He gave them a second chance. He told them stories about God. He healed and forgave them. When people got to know Jesus, they changed.

Scripture

LUKE 19:1–10

Zacchaeus

One day Jesus was going through the town of Jericho. The crowds gathered to see him. He did not plan to stop there. Now a man there named Zacchaeus, who was a chief tax collector and also a wealthy man, was seeking to see who Jesus was; but he could not see him because of the crowd, for he was short in stature. So he ran ahead and climbed a sycamore tree in order to see Jesus.

When he reached the place, Jesus looked up and said to him, "Zacchaeus, come down quickly, for today I must stay at your house." Zacchaeus came down quickly and welcomed Jesus to his house with joy.

The people in the crowd were not happy. They said, "He has gone to stay at the house of a sinner." They did not think Jesus should be around sinners.

Zacchaeus told Jesus, "I will give half of my possessions to the poor. If I have taken anything from anyone, I will pay them back four times more."

Jesus said, "Zacchaeus, today God's forgiveness has come to your house."

BASED ON LUKE 19:1–10

❓ **Why do you think Jesus decided to stay at Zacchaeus' house?**

❓ **How would you feel if Jesus came to your house? How would you change?**

Faith at Home

Read the scripture story with your family members. Discuss responses to the questions, and talk about how Zacchaeus changed after he met Jesus. Discuss ways your family welcomes people.

Share

Write a song   With a partner or in a small group, write words to the tune of "We Are Marching" that describe what you might do to welcome Jesus into your lives.

_____

_____

_____

_____

Second Chance

SIGNS OF FAITH

Reconciliation Room

The place where individuals celebrate the Sacrament of Reconciliation is called a **Reconciliation Room**. The room is set up so we can sit face-to-face with the priest, or we may choose to kneel or sit behind a screen while we speak to him. The priest cannot ever tell what we say to him during the Sacrament of Reconciliation.

Faith Focus

How are we welcomed in the Sacrament of Reconciliation?

When God created us, he gave us free will. This is the ability to choose between right and wrong. When we choose to do what we know is wrong, we sin.

One of the ways we can show we are sorry for our sins and ask God's forgiveness is in the **Sacrament of Reconciliation**. We also call this the **Sacrament of Penance**, the Sacrament of Forgiveness, or Confession.

We can celebrate this sacrament again and again. It is necessary to do so when we choose to completely turn away from God's love and separate ourselves from God's life. This is called a **mortal sin**. For a sin to be mortal, it must be seriously wrong, we must know it is seriously wrong, and we must freely choose to do it anyway. We can also celebrate this sacrament for less serious sins that weaken our friendship with God. A less serious sin is called a **venial sin**.

Preparation and Welcome

The Church celebrates Penance in two ways. In **individual celebrations** the person seeking forgiveness meets with the priest individually and in private. In **communal celebrations** groups of people gather to listen to God's word and pray together. Then each person tells his or her sins privately to the priest.

In the Sacrament of Reconciliation the priest acts in the place of Jesus. The priest is a sign of God's forgiveness. He prepares to welcome us to the Sacrament of Penance by praying to the Holy Spirit. He asks the Holy Spirit to help him tell us about God's love and forgiveness.

We prepare for the sacrament by praying to the Holy Spirit and looking at our actions. Whether we celebrate the Sacrament of Penance individually or as a group, we begin with the Sign of the Cross. Then the priest prays words like these:

> "May God who has enlightened every heart, help you to know your sins and trust in his mercy."

We answer, "Amen."

? **How will you ask the Holy Spirit to help you look at your life?**

Faith at Home

Discuss responses to the question on the page. Ask family members to share how they prepare to celebrate the Sacrament of Reconciliation. When you are at church this week, ask a family member to show you the Reconciliation Room.

Preparing to Celebrate

Respond

Create a sketch In the space below, create a sketch of ways you will prepare to celebrate the Sacrament of Reconciliation.

Closing Blessing

Gather and begin with the Sign of the Cross.

Leader: God, our Gracious Father, you welcome us as your children. Increase our faith and make us strong.

All: Hear us, we pray.

Leader: God, our Gracious Father, you call us to change and grow. Make our light burn brighter for you.

All: Hear us, we pray.

Leader: God, our Gracious Father, help us to know our sins and trust in your mercy.

All: Hear us, we pray.

♪ *Sing together.*

We are marching in the light
of God,
We are marching in the light
of God.
We are marching, we are marching
in the light of God.
We are marching, we are marching
in the light of God.

South African Traditional

Faith at Home

Faith Focus

- At Baptism we are called to walk in the light.

- Sin is a choice.

- The Sacrament of Reconciliation forgives sins committed after Baptism.

Ritual Focus
Renewal of Baptismal Promises

The celebration focused on the Renewal of Baptismal Promises. You renewed your baptismal promises and were sprinkled with holy water. During the week, use the text on pages 18–19 with your family members, and have them renew their baptismal promises with you.

Family Prayer

Loving Father, we give you thanks for all the ways you make yourself known to us. Help us to continue to spread the Light of Christ in our world. We ask this in the name of your Son, Jesus. Amen.

Act

Share Together Read Luke 19:1–10. Talk about what it must have been like for Zacchaeus to have Jesus come to his house and the changes he made after he met Jesus. Then invite family members to list people whose example caused them to change something in their own lives. Have each person read the names on his or her list. After each name, pray together, "God bless you for being a light in our life."

Do Together Together, think about and share the names of some people that your family could contribute some light and joy to. Remember that even small things can brighten someone's day. Choose one of the people, and plan what you will do to brighten his or her life.

3 We Reflect

We Gather

Procession

As you sing, walk forward slowly. Follow the person carrying the Bible.

 Sing together.

Misericordia, Señor, show us your mercy, O Lord, hemos pecado, for we have sinned.

Leader: Let us pray.

Make the Sign of the Cross together.

Ritual Focus: Reverencing the Word

Come forward one at a time. Bow or place your hand on the Bible.

Leader: [Name], may God's word always enlighten you.

Candidate: Amen.

Leader: God, our loving Father, you call us to holiness and goodness. You want us to be united in you. Send us the Holy Spirit so that our minds and hearts will be open to your word and the works of your goodness. We ask this through Jesus Christ our Lord.

All: Amen.

We Listen

Leader: A reading from the holy Gospel according to Luke.

All: Glory to you, Lord.

Leader: *Read Luke 10:25–28.* The Gospel of the Lord.

All: Praise to you, Lord Jesus Christ.

Sit silently.

Leader: Let us join in the prayer Jesus has taught us.

Pray the Lord's Prayer together.

We Go Forth

Leader: May the Lord bless us, protect us from all evil, and bring us to everlasting life.

All: Amen.

 Sing the opening song together.

God's Word

SIGNS OF FAITH

Bowing

Bending the head or body forward shows honor and adoration for God. We also bow in prayer when we want to ask for God's blessing. Sometimes we bow our heads to reverence the name of Jesus.

Reflect

Reverencing the word In the space provided, make a word collage using words that express your feelings about reverencing the Scriptures in the celebration. Also include words that describe the importance of God's word for you in your life.

God Speaks to Us

We reverence the Bible because it is a holy book. It is God's own word. The Bible tells the story of God's love for his people. The stories of what Jesus said and did are in the Bible.

We hear stories from the Bible every Sunday at Mass. During the Sacrament of Reconciliation, we read or listen to stories from the Bible. These stories may be about God's forgiveness or how we are to live God's laws.

We also use the Bible before we celebrate the Sacrament of Reconciliation to help us look at our lives. We pray to the Holy Spirit to help us know if we are living according to the Ten Commandments, the Beatitudes, the life of Jesus, and Church teachings.

SIGNS OF FAITH

The Bible

The Bible is God's own word. Another name used for the Bible is **Scriptures**. The word *Scriptures* means "writings." God inspired humans to write stories in the Bible about his love and forgiveness. The Bible has two parts, the Old Testament and the New Testament. The Old Testament tells the story of God's love and forgiveness before Jesus came. The New Testament tells us what Jesus and his followers taught about God's love and forgiveness.

Loving God and Neighbor

Faith Focus

What is the greatest commandment?

We want to do the right thing. Commandments help us know the difference between right and wrong. When Jesus was on earth, people wanted to know which one of God's commandments was the greatest.

Scripture

LUKE 10:25–28

The Great Commandment

One day when Jesus was teaching in a small town, there was a scholar of the law who stood up to test him, and said, "Teacher, what must I do to inherit eternal life?"

Jesus answered with a question of his own. "When you study God's law, what does it tell you?" The man replied, "You shall love the Lord your God with all your heart, with all your being, with all your strength, and with all your mind, and your neighbor as yourself." Jesus replied, "You have answered correctly. Do this and you will live."

BASED ON LUKE 10:25–28

The Ten Commandments sum up for us what is right and wrong. Out of love, God gave the Ten Commandments to the people of Israel and to us. Following the commandments helps people stay close to God.

The Ten Commandments are divided into the two parts of the Great Commandment. The first three commandments show us how we are to love God. The last seven show us how to love ourselves and others. When Jesus told the man he was right, he was telling him and us that the commandment of love is the greatest.

The Ten Commandments show us how to live as God wants us to live. They tell us how to love God, ourselves, and others. They show us the way to real happiness and eternal life.

? **What was Jesus trying to tell the man?**

? **When does following a commandment make you happy?**

Faith at Home

Read the scripture story with your family members. Discuss responses to the questions. Talk about situations in the family, school, or work where family members have to follow laws and rules. Talk about the positive results when everyone follows the laws or rules. Discuss how you as a family can live the Great Commandment.

Share

Role-play   With a partner or in a small group, brainstorm ways that young people today keep the Great Commandment. Plan a role-play about one of them, showing how a young person makes a choice to follow the commandment.

The Examination of Conscience

SIGNS OF FAITH

Precepts of the Church

Precepts of the Church are helpful laws made by the Church. They help us know the basic things we must do to grow in love of God and neighbor. A list of the precepts is on page 78.

Faith Focus

What happens during the examination of conscience?

When we prepare to receive the Sacrament of Reconciliation, we examine our conscience. Just as God gives us the gift of free will, he also gives us the gift of conscience. **Conscience** helps us know the difference between right and wrong, good and evil. It also helps us know whether something we already did was right or wrong. We strengthen our conscience when we pray for guidance and apply Jesus' teachings to our decision-making. Doing this helps our conscience point us in the right direction.

Here are some questions we ask ourselves during the **examination of conscience**:

- Did I live as Jesus wants me to?

- Did I go to Mass on Sunday?

- Did I love and respect my family members?

- Did I share my time and possessions with others?

- Did I tell the truth, return others' belongings, and treat people fairly?

We Listen to God's Word

When we examine our conscience, we can use Scripture. We often listen to Scripture during the celebration of the Sacrament of Reconciliation. When we receive the sacrament individually, the priest may read the Scripture. Or he may ask us to read a scripture story.

When we celebrate the sacrament with the community, we begin with a Celebration of the Word of God. We listen to one or more readings, and the priest gives a homily. The readings and homily help us hear God's voice. They remind us that God wants to forgive us.

After the homily there is a period of silence. We prayerfully think about our lives.

 Which scripture story will you choose for your examination of conscience?

Faith at Home

Share the scripture story you chose with family members. Ask them to share one that they might use. Using page 81 of this book, go over the guidelines for the examination of conscience with family members.

Showing Love

Respond

Create a reminder In the space provided write ten ways you will keep the commandments this week. You can use a commandment more than once. Keep the list as a reminder for the week.

How I will live the Commandments

1. _____
   _____
2. _____
   _____
3. _____
   _____
4. _____
   _____
5. _____
   _____

6. _____
   _____
7. _____
   _____
8. _____
   _____
9. _____
   _____
10. _____
    _____

Closing Blessing

Gather and begin with the Sign of the Cross.

Leader: The Lord speaks words of forgiveness and love always. Let us ask him to open our minds and hearts to his love.

All: We pray you, hear us.

Leader: Teach us your ways, O Lord, that we may follow your commandments.

All: We pray you, hear us.

Leader: Open our hearts to your word, that we will learn to follow it and grow ever closer to you.

All: We pray you, hear us.

🎵 *Sing together.*

Misericordia, Señor, show us your mercy, O Lord,
hemos pecado, for we have sinned.

© 1998, Bob Hurd. Published by OCP

Faith at Home

Faith Focus

- We prepare for the Sacrament of Reconciliation with an examination of conscience, using the word of God.

- The Holy Spirit guides us in examining our conscience.

- Conscience is the ability to know right from wrong.

Ritual Focus
Reverencing the Word

The celebration focused on Reverencing the Word. You honored God's word by bowing before the Bible or placing your hand on it, while the catechist prayed that God's word would enlighten you. During the week, spend some time each day reading from the Bible. If you do not have a Bible, use the scripture stories in your book.

Family Prayer

God, our Father, thank you for giving us the gift of conscience. Help us to be kind and helpful to one another. Make us a family that loves you and all the people in our lives. Amen.

Act

Share Together With your family, watch a favorite video, movie, or TV show. Afterward, discuss how the characters were or were not living the Great Commandment. Ask other family members to share examples of people they know who live this commandment in their daily lives.

Do Together Ask your family members to do an examination of conscience together. Read the scripture reading from this lesson. Invite family members to name times when one of you lived the Great Commandment. Decide one way your family will live out this commandment in the next week. Conclude by praying the Lord's Prayer together.

GO ONLINE **www.harcourtreligion.com**
Visit our Web site for weekly scripture readings and questions, family resources, and more activities.

CHAPTER 4

We Are Sorry

We Gather

Procession

As you sing, walk forward slowly. Follow the person carrying the Bible.

🎵 *Sing together.*

Remember your love and
  your faithfulness, O Lord.
Remember your people and
  have mercy on us, Lord.

© 1978, Damean Music.
Distributed by GIA Publications

Leader: Let us pray.

Make the Sign of the Cross together.

We Listen

Leader: Loving Father, send us the Holy Spirit to open our ears and hearts that we may hear your word and be filled with the courage to live it. We ask this through Jesus Christ our Lord.

All: Amen.

Leader: A reading from the holy Gospel according to Luke.

All: Glory to you, Lord.

Leader: *Read Luke 7:36–38, 44–48, 50*
The Gospel of the Lord.

All: Praise to you, Lord Jesus Christ.

Sit silently.

Ritual Focus: Examination of Conscience and Act of Contrition

Leader: The sinful woman showed sorrow. Let us think about what we are sorry for.

Use these questions to examine your conscience.

Did I love and honor God?

Did I keep Sunday as a holy day?

Did I obey my parents?

Did I share with others?

Was I kind to others?

Did I tell the truth?

Let us now kneel and pray the Act of Contrition.

All: My God, I am sorry for my sins with all my heart. In choosing to do wrong and failing to do good, I have sinned against you, whom I should love above all things. I firmly intend, with your help, to do penance, to sin no more, and to avoid whatever leads me to sin. Our Savior Jesus Christ suffered and died for us. In his name, my God, have mercy. Amen.

Stand.

We Go Forth

Leader: Lord, our God, you know all things. We want to be more generous in serving you.

All: Amen.

Sing the opening song together.

Sorrow for Sin

SIGNS OF FAITH

Kneeling

Kneeling is a way we pray with our bodies. When we get on our knees, we are telling God that he is important to us. We depend on him. Kneeling is also a way of saying we are sorry for our sins and we want to be forgiven. It is a prayer of **penitence**.

Reflect

Examination of conscience and Act of Contrition   Write a paragraph about the celebration. Include how you felt as you examined your conscience and knelt for the Act of Contrition. In your last two sentences, tell something you learned about God, yourself, or the Church in this celebration.

_____

_____

_____

_____

_____

_____

_____

_____

_____

Ask for Forgiveness

When we are unkind to our friends or our family, we hurt our friendship with them, and we feel sorrow or sadness. We wish we did not act that way. We want to make things right. We tell them we are sorry for what we did. We promise not do it again. We make up.

When we sin, we do things that hurt our friendship with God and others. When we examine our conscience, we pray to the Holy Spirit. The Holy Spirit helps us remember how much God loves us. We remember what a good friend Jesus is. We think about the ways we have hurt our friendship with God and others. The Holy Spirit helps us to be sorry for our sins. The Holy Spirit helps us say to God and to others. "I am sorry. Please forgive me."

Contrition

Contrition is sorrow for sin. It is the first and most important action in the Sacrament of Penance. There are different kinds of contrition. Perfect contrition is when we are sorry for our sins because we have ignored or turned away from God. Sometimes we're sorry because of how much we love God. Other times we are sorry because we are ashamed of what we did. Imperfect contrition is when we are sorry for our sins for reasons other than our love for God, such as fear of punishment. Both kinds of contrition are gifts of the Holy Spirit. We must have sorrow for our sins to receive the grace of the sacrament.

Sinners Come to Jesus

Faith Focus

How do people tell Jesus they are sorry?

When people heard Jesus' good news about God's love, they were sorry for their sins. They wanted to tell him how sorry they were.

Scripture

LUKE 7:36–38, 44–48, 50

A Woman Who Was Sorry

Simon, a Pharisee, invited Jesus to have dinner with him. So Jesus went to his home and reclined at the table.

Now there was a sinful woman in the city who learned that he was at the table in the house of the Pharisee. Bringing an alabaster flask of ointment, she knelt at his feet weeping and began to bathe his feet with her tears. Then she wiped them with her hair, kissed them, and anointed them with the ointment.

When the Pharisee who had invited him saw this he said to himself, "If this man were a prophet, he would know who and what sort of woman this is who is touching him, that she is a sinner."

Jesus said to Simon, "Simon, I have something to say to you. When I came into your home, you did not give me water to clean my feet. But this woman has washed my feet with her tears and dried them with her hair. You did not greet me with a kiss, but she has not stopped kissing my feet. You did not anoint my head with oil but she anointed my feet with expensive oil. So I tell you, her many sins have been forgiven. She has shown great love."

Then Jesus said to the woman, "Your sins are forgiven. Your faith has saved you. Go in peace."

BASED ON LUKE 7:36–38, 44-48, 50

? How did the woman show Jesus she was sorry for her sins?

? How do you tell Jesus you are sorry?

Faith at Home

Read the scripture story with your family members. Discuss the responses to the questions. Talk about the different ways there are to say "I am sorry."

Share

Write a prayer On a separate piece of paper, write your own prayer of sorrow to Jesus.

The Confession of Sin

SIGNS OF FAITH

Penitent

A person who confesses sin during the Rite of Penance is called a **penitent**.

Faith Focus

Why do we confess our sins?

The woman in the scripture story showed Jesus she was sorry for her sins through her actions. In the Sacrament of Reconciliation, the Church gives us a wonderful way to show our sorrow for our sins. The Sacrament includes each of these four things.

- We admit we have done something wrong. This is called **confession**. We must always confess our mortal sins before going to communion. It is good for us to confess our venial sins often. Confession always helps our friendship with God grow stronger.

- We say "I am sorry." This is called **contrition**.

- We plan so we will not act unlovingly the next time. This is called a firm purpose of amendment.

- We do the prayer or action the priest tells us to do. This is called doing a **penance**.

Sorrow and Penance

In the Sacrament of Reconciliation, we confess our sins to the priest. He is called the **confessor**. The priest acts as God's minister when he listens to our confession. We talk with the priest about how we can make things better.

Then the priest gives us a penance. A penance is a prayer or action that we do to show we are really sorry. The penance may be doing a good act connected to the sin, such as returning stolen property. It may also be an action that shows that we are willing to change, such as being kind. Often it is saying prayers.

Doing the penance helps us take responsibility for our actions. It reminds us to think about how our choices might hurt others.

After we accept our penance, we pray an **Act of Contrition**. The Act of Contrition is a prayer of sorrow. We tell God we are sorry and want to do better. We ask God to help us avoid temptation.

Faith at Home

Discuss your response to the question on this page with family members. Ask them to share their thoughts. Discuss what the difference is between someone just saying the words "I am sorry" and someone showing that they are really sorry. Ask a family member to help you learn the Act of Contrition on page 39.

? **How does confession help us?**

Showing Sorrow

Respond

Make a card   Think about someone to whom you need to say "I am sorry." Use art materials to make a card that expresses your sorrow. Use the space below to brainstorm and to outline how you want to express your sorrow. Decide how and when you will deliver the card.

Closing Blessing

Gather and begin with the Sign of the Cross.

Leader: Lord, look on us and hear our prayer. Give us strength to turn away from sin.

All: Lord, hear our prayer.

Leader: Help us to be sorry for our sins and to change so we can be better followers of Jesus.

All: Lord, hear our prayer.

Leader: Help us to trust in your goodness and to be your generous children.

All: Lord, hear our prayer.

♪ *Sing together.*

Remember your love and your faithfulness, O Lord.
Remember your people and have mercy on us, Lord.

Faith at Home

Faith Focus

- The Holy Spirit helps us to be sorry for our sins.

- Sorrow for sin is very important part of the Sacrament of Reconciliation.

- A penance is a prayer or action given by the priest that we do to show we are sorry for what we have done.

Ritual Focus
Examination of Conscience and Act of Contrition

The celebration focused on the examination of conscience and Act of Contrition. You spent quiet time thinking about your own actions. This week spend some quiet time with a family member, and together use the questions on page 39 to review each day. Begin your quiet time with the prayer to the Holy Spirit on page 80.

Family Prayer

Loving Father, send your Holy Spirit to help us understand when our actions hurt others in our family. Give us the strength to tell God and one another we are are sorry and to do better in the future. We ask this in Jesus' name. Amen.

Act

Share Together All of us use the phrase "I'm sorry." It can mean many things. We use it when we bump into someone. We use it when we have hurt someone. We use it when we experience loss. We use it to respond to someone when they tell us something sad. Ask family members to discuss together all the different meanings of the words "I'm sorry." Have family members share stories of how they let people know they were sorry and what happened after they expressed their sorrow.

Do Together Read the Act of Contrition on page 39 with your family members. Discuss each phrase of the prayer and share examples of what each phrase means. Then pray the Act of Contrition together.

GO ONLINE **www.harcourtreligion.com**
Visit our Web site for weekly scripture readings and questions, family resources, and more activities.

5 We Are Forgiven

We Gather

Procession

*As you sing, walk forward slowly.
Follow the person carrying the
Bible.*

🎼 *Sing together.*

Children of God in one
   family,
loved by God in one family.
And no matter what we do
God loves me and God
   loves you.

© 1998, Christopher Walker.
Published by OCP Publications

Leader: Let us pray.

*Make the Sign of
the Cross.*

We Listen

Leader: Good and gracious Father, you
who are always ready to forgive
us, send us the Holy Spirit. Open
our hearts and minds to know
your forgiving love. We ask this
in the name of your Son, Jesus.

Leader: A reading from the holy Gospel
according to Luke.

Leader: *Read Luke 15:11–32.*

The Gospel of the Lord.

All: Praise to you, Lord Jesus Christ.

Sit silently.

Ritual Focus: Prayer over the Candidates

Leader: In the scripture story Jesus told us a story about a father who loved his son very much.

Come forward to the prayer table.

Place your open hands on the head of each candidate.

[Name], God loves you and will always forgive you.

Candidate: Thanks be to God.

Leader: Let us ask God our Father to forgive us and free us from evil.

Pray the Lord's Prayer together.

We Go Forth

Leader: May the God of peace fill your hearts with every blessing. May he strengthen you with the gift of hope. May he grant you all that is good.

All: Amen.

🎼 *Sing the opening song together.*

Reconciliation

Signs of Faith

Laying on of Hands
Jesus used the gesture of laying hands on people when he was blessing or healing them. In the Sacrament of Reconciliation, the priest extends his hands or hand over the head of the penitent as he prays the prayer of forgiveness.

Reflect

Prayer over the candidates Think about the celebration, and complete the following statements with your own thoughts and feelings.

When people pray for me

_____

_____

When I heard the words "God loves you and will always forgive you"

_____

_____

_____

The Lord's Prayer reminds me

_____

_____

Brought Together Again

When we are unkind to others, we hurt our relationship with them. Our parents, grandparents, teachers, or others in authority trust us to obey them. When we disobey them they are disappointed in us.

Sometimes we do things that hurt our friendship with others and we want to make it better. We say "I am sorry." But we cannot make it better all by ourselves. The people we disobey or hurt have to forgive us. When they say "I forgive you," we are one with them again. We are reconciled. **Reconciliation** means "to bring together again, or reunite."

In the Sacrament of Penance, God is always ready to forgive us. Through the power of the Holy Spirit we are reconciled with God and one another.

SIGNS OF FAITH

Heaven

God wants us to be one with him. This is why he forgives us. People who do not confess mortal sins will be separated from God forever. God wants us to be happy with him forever in heaven. So we confess our sins and try to grow in holiness now. People who die in God's friendship will eventually share in the joy of heaven.

God Wants to Forgive

Faith Focus

What does Jesus tell us about God's forgiveness?

Jesus welcomed sinners. He ate and drank with them. He healed them and he forgave their sins. He also told stories to help the people understand how much God, his Father, wanted to forgive them. Jesus once told this story:

Scripture

LUKE 15:11–24

The Forgiving Father

A man had two sons, and the younger son said to his father, "Father, give me the share of your estate that should come to me." So the father divided the property between them.

After a few days, the younger son collected all his belongings and set off to a distant country where he squandered his inheritance on foolish things. When he had freely spent everything, a severe famine struck that country and he found himself in dire need.

So he hired himself out to one of the local citizens who sent him to his farm to tend the pigs. And he longed to eat his fill of the pods on which the swine fed, but nobody gave him any. Coming to his senses he thought, "How many of my father's hired workers have more than enough to eat,

52

but here am I, dying from hunger. I shall get up and go to my father and I shall say to him. 'Father, I have sinned against heaven and against you. I no longer deserve to be called your son; treat me as you would treat one of your hired workers.'"

So he got up and went back to his father. While he was still a long way off, his father caught sight of him, and was filled with compassion. He ran to his son, embraced him, and kissed him. His son said to him, "Father, I have sinned against heaven and against you; I no longer deserve to be called your son."

But his father told the servants, "Quickly bring the finest robe and put it on him; put a ring on his finger and sandals on his feet. Take the fattened calf and slaughter it. Then let us celebrate with a feast, because this son of mine was dead, and has come to life again; he was lost, and has been found." Then the celebration began.

BASED ON LUKE 15:11–24

? **What do you think the father will do?**

? **What does this story tell you about God?**

Faith at Home

Read the scripture story with your family members. Discuss the responses to both questions. Talk about why forgiveness is sometimes difficult.

Share

Create a story Jesus' story of the Forgiving Father describes what God's forgiveness is like. With a partner or small group, create a modern-day story that describes God's forgiveness.

The Sacrament of Forgiveness

SIGNS OF FAITH

Purple Stole

A **stole** is a vestment the priest wears when celebrating the sacraments. It is a sign of his obedience to God and his priestly authority. During the Sacrament of Reconciliation, the priest wears a purple stole around his neck and over his shoulders. The color purple is a sign of penance.

Faith Focus

How are sins forgiven in the Sacrament of Reconciliation?

In the scripture story, the son tells his father what he has done wrong and asks forgiveness. The father forgives the son and then surprises him. He brings him back into the family. The son is reconciled.

There are many ways we share in God's forgiveness. The most important ways are in the sacraments, especially the Sacrament of Reconciliation. The Sacrament of Reconciliation does just what it says:

- It forgives our sins.

- It brings us back together with God in friendship.

- It brings us back to the Church and makes us stronger members.

- It brings us peace.

- It heals our relationships.

- It makes us one with all creation.

Forgiveness and Absolution

God forgives our sins in the Sacrament of Reconciliation through the ministry of the priest. After we confess our sins, accept our penance, and pray an Act of Contrition, the priest extends his hands over us and prays this prayer of forgiveness:

"God, the Father of mercies,
through the death and resurrection of his Son
has reconciled the world to himself
and sent the Holy Spirit among us
for the forgiveness of sins;
through the ministry of the Church
may God give you pardon and peace,
and I absolve you from your sins
in the name of the Father, and of the Son,
and of the Holy Spirit."

RITE OF PENANCE, 55

This prayer is the prayer of **absolution**. *Absolution* means "forgiveness." We receive God's forgiveness through the Church in the Sacrament of Reconciliation.

? **What happens in the Sacrament of Reconciliation?**

Faith at Home

With your family members, talk about each of the effects of the Sacrament of Reconciliation on page 54. Review your response to the question on this page with them. Ask a family member to review the Rite of Reconciliation with you. Use pages 74–75 in this book.

Serving Others

Respond

Be a forgiving person Think of someone you need to forgive. Write what you will do to show him or her forgiveness this week.

_____

_____

_____

_____

_____

_____

_____

_____

_____

Closing Blessing

Gather and begin with the Sign of the Cross.

Leader: God, our Father, in your goodness forgive us our sins.

All: Lord, hear our prayer.

Leader: Jesus, our Savior, welcome us and show us your mercy.

All: Lord, hear our prayer.

Leader: Holy Spirit, fill us with the gift of forgiveness that we may forgive others as we are forgiven.

All: Lord, hear our prayer.

♪ *Sing together.*

Children of God in one family,
loved by God in one family.
And no matter what we do
God loves me and God
    loves you.

Faith at Home

Faith Focus

- In the Sacrament of Reconciliation, God is always ready to forgive us.

- God wants us to be one with him. Reconciliation means "to bring together again, or reunite."

- Through the power of the Holy Spirit and the ministry of the priest, our sins are forgiven.

Ritual Focus
Prayer over the Candidates

The celebration focused on God's love and forgiveness. You came forward and the catechist extended his or her hands and prayed, reminding you that God loves and forgives you. Then you prayed the Lord's Prayer. Every day during the week, take the time to pray the Lord's Prayer slowly, and think about each verse.

Family Prayer

Dear God,
You are so generous in your love for us. You always welcome us back. Help us to be generous in our forgiveness of others. Amen.

Act

Share Together Together read the three stories in Chapter 15 of the Gospel of Luke. Spend a few minutes explaining that Jesus told these stories to show how much God loves sinners and wants to forgive them. Have family members share their responses to the following questions: What is Jesus telling us about God in these stories? Which of the three stories do you like the best? Why?

Do Together As a family group, share some stories of times individual family members experienced being forgiven or forgiving someone else. Talk about times it is hard to forgive others. Prayerfully read Luke 15:11–24. Together write a prayer asking the Holy Spirit to help you to be forgiving to one another. Place the prayer in an area of your home where family members will see it during the next week. Pray the prayer together at appropriate times during the week, such as when you gather for meals, at bedtime, or before a family gathering.

GO ONLINE **www.harcourtreligion.com**
Visit our Web site for weekly scripture readings and questions, family resources, and more activities.

6 We Go Forth

We Gather

Procession

As you sing, walk forward slowly. Follow the person carrying the Bible.

🎵 *Sing together.*

We're all coming back
　　together
With our God and family.
We're all coming back
　　together
Building the kingdom with
　　everyone.
Building the kingdom with
　　everyone.

© 2000 John Burland

Leader:　Let us pray.

Make the Sign of the Cross together.

We Listen

Leader:　Loving Father, we come together in your presence to remember that we are your children. You call us to be children of light. Open our hearts to the Holy Spirit that we will understand your word. We ask this through Jesus Christ our Lord.

All:　Amen.

Leader:　A reading from the holy Gospel according to John.

All:　Glory to you, Lord.

Leader:　*Read John 20:19–23.*
　　The Gospel of the Lord.

All:　Praise to you, Lord Jesus Christ.

Sit silently.

Ritual Focus: Sprinkling with Holy Water and the Sign of Peace

Leader: Jesus asks us to forgive others and to bring peace into the world. Through our Baptism and the Sacrament of Reconciliation, we are freed from sin and evil.

All: Amen

Leader: *Sprinkle the candidates with water.*
You have been baptized in Christ and called to bring his light to the world.

All: Amen. Alleluia!

Leader: Let us offer one another the Sign of Peace.

Offer one another a sign of Christ's peace.

Say: The Peace of the Lord be with you.

Answer: And also with you.

We Go Forth

Leader: God, our Father, send us the Holy Spirit, the giver of peace that we may go forth as a people of peace and forgiveness.

All: Thanks be to God.

 Sing the opening song together.

We Share

SIGNS OF FAITH

Sprinkling with Holy Water

At some Sunday Masses during the year, the priest walks through the church and sprinkles the assembly with holy water. The sprinkling reminds us of our Baptism. In Baptism, God forgives and heals us. When the priest does the sprinkling with water, it takes the place of the Penitential Rite.

Reflect

Sprinkling with Holy Water and the Sign of Peace   In the celebration you heard the words "you have been baptized in Christ and you are called to bring his light to the world." In a paragraph, describe what those words mean for you. Include an example of how you bring Christ's light to others.

_____

_____

_____

_____

_____

_____

_____

_____

_____

_____

We Are Reconciled

We grow and change when we celebrate the Sacrament of Reconciliation. The Sacrament of Reconciliation is a sacrament of **conversion**. *Conversion* means "to change or to move away from one thing and toward another."

When we celebrate the Sacrament of Reconciliation, we name the things that have broken or hurt our relationship with God and others. We are sorry and we want to change. We want to move away from the actions that keep us from growing as a child of light. We accept the penance the priest gives us to show that we want to change.

We receive God's forgiveness and peace. Through the action of the Holy Spirit, we are one again with God and others. We are reconciled and at peace.

Sign of Peace
During the Mass we exchange the Sign of Peace before Communion. The Sign of Peace is a sacred action. It is a sign that we are one in the Body of Christ. When we offer each other the Sign of Peace, we remember that we are all one.

Hear God's Word

Faith Focus

What did Jesus send the disciples to do?

While he was alive, Jesus' disciples traveled, preaching and healing in his name. The Risen Jesus wanted his followers to continue to carry on his work of healing and forgiveness.

Scripture

JOHN 20:19–23

Jesus Appears to the Disciples

On the evening of that first day of the week, the disciples were in a room with locked doors, for fear of the Jews. Then, Jesus came and stood in their midst and said to them, "Peace be with you."

When he had said this, he showed them his hands and his side. The disciples rejoiced when they saw the Lord.

Jesus said to them again, "Peace be with you. As the Father has sent me, so I send you."

And when he said this, he breathed on them and said to them, "Receive the Holy Spirit.

"Whose sins you forgive are forgiven them, and whose sins you retain are retained."

BASED ON JOHN 20:19–23

? **What is Jesus sending the disciples to do?**

? **How do you show forgiveness and peace to others?**

Faith at Home

Read the scripture story with your family members. Discuss your responses to the questions. Talk about ways forgiveness brings peace. Use examples from your family's life together.

Share

Write slogans With a partner or a small group, create slogans about living as forgiving and reconciling people. Write your slogan on a large sheet of paper and hang it in a conspicuous place.

Proclamation of Praise and Dismissal

SIGNS OF FAITH

Bishops and Priests
In a special way the Church continues Jesus' mission of forgiveness and reconciliation through the ministry of priests and bishops. Like the Apostles, bishops and priests receive from Jesus the authority to absolve people from their sins. They teach us how to live out the mission of reconciliation.

Faith Focus

How do we share reconciliation with others?

Jesus wanted his disciples to know they were forgiven. He wanted them to be at peace. He also wanted them to know they had a special job, a mission. He was sending them to make the world a better place. He wanted them to bring forgiveness and peace to others just as he did in his life. He was calling them to be reconcilers.

The Church continues the mission of reconciliation today. We are reconcilers when we:

- forgive others
- ask for forgiveness
- are fair to others
- act with kindness
- share what we have with those who do not have
- respect all people because they are God's children

The mission of reconciliation is not always easy, but the Holy Spirit gives us strength and courage to carry it out.

Go Forth

At the end of the celebration of Reconciliation, we give praise to God for his wonderful gift of forgiveness and reconciliation.

After the prayer of absolution the priest says, "Give thanks to the Lord, for he is good." We respond, "His mercy endures for ever." Then the priest sends us forth. He says this or a similar blessing:

> "Go in peace,
> and proclaim to the world
> the wonderful works of God
> who has brought you salvation."

RITE OF PENANCE, 47

Our sins are forgiven in the Sacrament of Reconciliation. The Holy Spirit remains with us to help us grow and become more like Jesus. This is such a great gift. We want to tell the world about it. The best way we can do that is to be living signs of God's forgiveness and reconciliation to others.

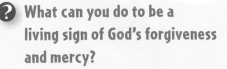

Faith at Home

Review your response to the question with family members and then invite others to share. Go over the meaning of reconciliation on page 72 in this book.

? **What can you do to be a living sign of God's forgiveness and mercy?**

Being a Reconciler

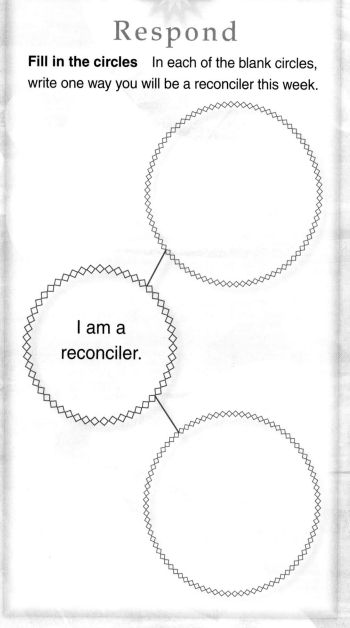

Respond

Fill in the circles   In each of the blank circles, write one way you will be a reconciler this week.

I am a reconciler.

Closing Blessing

Gather and begin with the Sign of the Cross.

Leader: God and Father of us all, forgive our sins.

All: Thank you for your forgiveness.

Leader: Jesus, our Savior, give us the gift of peace.

All: Thank you for your peace.

Leader: Holy Spirit, give us your strength and courage.

All: Thank you for your strength and courage.

Sing together.

We're all coming back together
With our God and family.
We're all coming back together
Building the kingdom with
    everyone.
Building the kingdom with
    everyone.

© 2000 John Burland

Faith at Home

Faith Focus

- The Sacrament of Reconciliation is a sacrament of conversion.

- The mission of reconciliation is to bring forgiveness and peace to others.

- The Holy Spirit remains with us to help us grow and become more like Jesus.

Ritual Focus
Sprinkling with Holy Water and the Sign of Peace

The celebration focused on bringing Christ's light and peace into the world. You were sprinkled with water and extended a Sign of Peace to one another. During the week, be aware of situations where you can bring peace to others.

Family Prayer

Gracious God, we give you thanks and praise for the gifts of your mercy and forgiveness. Help us to go out and spread the word of your love to those we meet. Show us how to be reconcilers in our family and with our friends.

Act

Share Together Have family members share their best experiences of the Sacrament of Reconciliation. Read John 20:19–23, and discuss how the disciples must have felt when Jesus appeared to them after the Resurrection. He just says "Peace be with you." Invite family members to share any stories or memories of people they know who forgive like Jesus did. Conclude the sharing with the Prayer of Saint Francis on page 80 of this book.

Do Together For the next week, gather at an appropriate time each day such as at mealtime, before bedtime, or before an evening activity. Light a candle. (This might be a good time to burn your Baptismal candle.) Pray this prayer: We have been baptized in Christ and are called to bring his light to the world. Then have family members share one way they were a light to someone during the day. Together, pray the Prayer to the Holy Spirit on page 80 of this book.

GO ONLINE www.harcourtreligion.com
Visit our Web site for weekly scripture readings and questions, family resources, and more activities.

Catholic Source Book

Words of Faith

absolution The forgiveness of sin that we receive from God through the Church in the Sacrament of Reconciliation.

Baptism The sacrament that makes the person a child of God and a member of the Church. It takes away original sin and all personal sin and makes the person a temple of the Holy Spirit.

communal celebration In a communal celebration, the assembly gathers to pray and hear God's word. Each penitent then confesses his or her sins to a priest, receives a penance, and is absolved individually.

confession Telling our sins to a priest in the Sacrament of Reconciliation. What we confess to the priest is private.

confessor A priest who acts as God's minister when he listens to our confession.

conscience God's gift which helps us know the difference between right and wrong. It also helps us recognize whether an action we already did was right or wrong.

contrition Sorrow for sins and a willingness to do better. Contrition is our first step toward forgiveness. As part of the Sacrament of Reconciliation, we pray an Act or Prayer of Contrition.

conversion A sincere change of mind, will, and heart away from sin and toward God. The Sacrament of Reconciliation is a sacrament of conversion.

examination of conscience A prayerful way of looking at our lives in light of the Ten Commandments, the Beatitudes, the life of Jesus, and the teachings of the Church. It helps us know whether what we have done is right or wrong.

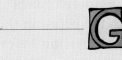

grace A sharing in God's own life.

Holy Trinity The three Persons in one God: God the Father, God the Son, and God the Holy Spirit.

holy water Water blessed by the priest for a religious purpose.

individual celebration In an individual celebration, the penitent meets with the priest in the Reconciliation room. The penitent confesses his or her sins to the priest, receives a penance, and is absolved.

mortal sin A serious sin that separates us from God's life.

original sin The name given to the first sin of humans. Because they disobeyed God and turned away from his friendship, original sin is passed to all of us.

Paschal candle A candle that is blessed at Easter Vigil and is burned during the Masses of the Easter season. It is also burned at Baptisms and funerals throughout the year.

penance A prayer or good action that we do to show we are sorry for our sins and want to do better. In the Sacrament of Reconciliation, the priest gives us a penance.

penitent The person who confesses his or her sins to the priest in the Sacrament of Reconciliation.

Precepts of the Church Laws of the Church that help us know what we should do to grow in love of God and neighbor.

priest A man who is ordained to serve God and the Church by celebrating the sacraments, preaching, and presiding at Mass. The priest is the confessor, or minister of the Sacrament of Reconciliation. The stole is a sign of the priest's obedience to God and of his priestly authority.

R

reconciliation A coming back together.

Reconciliation room A room or chapel in which the confessor, or priest, hears the penitent's confession of sins. The room is usually furnished with chairs, a kneeler, a table for the Bible, and a candle. A movable screen can also be used as a divider between the priest and the penitent.

S

sacrament A holy sign that comes from Jesus and gives us grace, a share in God's life.

Sacrament of Penance Another name for the Sacrament of Reconciliation.

Sacrament of Reconciliation A sacrament of forgiveness through which the sinner is reconciled with God and the Church.

Scriptures The word of God contained in the Bible. The word *Scripture* means "holy writing." Scripture is used for reflecting on God's love and forgiveness in the Sacrament of Reconciliation. Scripture is proclaimed by a lector or reader, at Mass, at a communal celebration, or in other liturgical celebrations.

sin The choice to disobey God. Sin is a deliberate choice, not a mistake or accident. We accept God's loving forgiveness for our sins when we show by our sorrow that we are willing to do better.

stole A vestment the priest wears around his neck when celebrating the sacraments.

venial sin A less serious sin that weakens our friendship with God.

Celebrating the Sacrament

The Communal Rite of Reconciliation

Before celebrating the Sacrament of Reconciliation, take time to examine your conscience. Pray for the Holy Spirit's help.

1. Introductory Rites

Join in singing the opening hymn. The priest will greet the assembly and lead you in the opening prayer.

2. Celebration of the Word of God

Listen to the word of God. There may be more than one reading, with a hymn or psalm in between. The last reading will be from one of the Gospels.

3. Homily

Listen as the priest helps you understand the meaning of the Scriptures.

4. Examination of Conscience, Litany, and the Lord's Prayer

After the homily there will be a time of silence. The priest may lead the assembly in an examination of conscience. This will be followed by a prayer of confession and a litany or song. Then everyone prays the Lord's Prayer together.

5. Individual Confession, Giving of Penance, and Absolution

While you wait to talk with the priest, you may pray quietly or join in singing. When it is your turn, confess your sins to the priest. He will talk to you about how to do better. He will give you a penance and extend his hands over your head and pray the prayer of absolution.

6. Proclamation of Praise and Dismissal

After everyone has confessed individually, join in the prayer or in singing a litany of thanksgiving. The priest or deacon will lead the closing prayer and bless the assembly. Then the priest or deacon will dismiss the assembly.

After celebrating the sacrament, carry out your penance as soon as possible.

The Individual Rite of Reconciliation

Before celebrating the Sacrament of Reconciliation, take time to examine your conscience. Pray for the Holy Spirit's help.

Wait for your turn to enter the Reconciliation room. You may choose to meet with the priest face-to-face or be separated from the priest by a screen.

1. Welcome

The priest will welcome you and invite you to pray the Sign of the Cross.

2. Reading of the Word of God

The priest may read or recite a passage from the Bible. You may be invited by the priest to read the Scripture yourself.

3. Confession of Sins and Giving of Penance

You tell your sins to the priest. The priest will talk with you about how to do better. Then the priest will give you a penance.

4. Prayer of the Penitent

Pray an Act of Contrition.

5. Absolution

The priest will hold his hand over your head and pray the prayer of absolution. As he says the final words, he will make the Sign of the Cross.

6. Proclamation of Praise and Dismissal

You and the priest praise God for his mercy, and the priest sends you forth.

After celebrating the Sacrament, carry out your penance as soon as possible.

Remember, after you celebrate this sacrament for the first time, you should receive it often to strengthen your friendship with God. We receive the Sacrament of Reconciliation before we receive Holy Communion for the first time. We are required to celebrate the Sacrament of Reconciliation once a year, if we have committed mortal sin. We cannot receive Holy Communion if we have not received forgiveness for a mortal sin.

Sources of Morality

The Great Commandment

"You shall love the Lord your God with all your heart, and with all your soul, and with all your strength, and with all your mind; and your neighbor as yourself."

Luke 10:27

The New Commandment

"This is my commandment, that you love one another as I have loved you."

John 15:12

Love of Enemies

"But I say to you, Love your enemies and pray for those who persecute you, so that you may be children of your Father in heaven...."

Matthew 5:44–45

The Beatitudes

"Blessed are the poor in spirit,
for theirs is the kingdom of heaven.

Blessed are those who mourn,
for they will be comforted.

Blessed are the meek,
for they will inherit the earth.

Blessed are those who hunger and thirst
for righteousness,
for they will be filled.

Blessed are the merciful,
for they will receive mercy.

Blessed are the pure in heart,
for they will see God.

Blessed are the peacemakers,
for they will be called children of God.

Blessed are those who are persecuted for
righteousness' sake,
for theirs is the kingdom of heaven."

Matthew 5:3–10

Catholic Prayers

The Sign of the Cross

In the name of the Father
and of the Son
and of the Holy Spirit
Amen.

The Lord's Prayer

Our Father, who art in heaven,
hallowed be thy name;
thy kingdom come;
thy will be done on earth as it is in
    heaven.
Give us this day our daily bread;
and forgive us our trespasses
as we forgive those who trespass
    against us;
and lead us not into temptation,
But deliver us from evil.
Amen.

Act of Contrition

My God,
I am sorry for my sins with all my heart.
In choosing to do wrong
and failing to do good,
I have sinned against you
whom I should love above all things.
I firmly intend, with your help,
to do penance,
to sin no more,
and to avoid whatever leads me to sin.
Our Savior Jesus Christ
suffered and died for us.
In his name, my God, have mercy.

Confiteor

I confess to Almighty God
and to you, my brothers and sisters,
that I have sinned through my own fault,
in my thoughts and in my words,
in what I have done,
and in what I have failed to do;
and I ask Blessed Mary ever virgin,
all the angels and saints,
and you, my brothers and sisters,
to pray for me to the Lord our God.

Prayer of Saint Francis of Assisi

Lord, make me an instrument of your
    peace.
Where there is hatred, let me show
    love;
where there is injury, pardon;
where there is doubt, faith;
where there is despair, hope;
where there is darkness, light;
and where there is sadness, joy.

O Divine Master, grant that I may not
    so much seek
to be consoled as to console;
to be understood as to understand;
to be loved as to love.
For it is in giving that we receive;
it is in pardoning that we are
    pardoned;
and it is in dying that we are born to
    eternal life.
Amen.

Prayer to the Holy Spirit

Come, Holy Spirit, fill the hearts of
    your faithful
And kindle in them the fire of your
    love.
Send forth your Spirit and they shall
    be created.
And you shall renew the face of the
    earth.

An Examination of Conscience

1. You prepare for the Sacrament of Reconciliation by thinking about the things you have done or not done. Think about how you have followed the Beatitudes, the Ten Commandments, and the Great Commandment.

2. Pray to the Holy Spirit to be with you as you think about your choices and actions.

3. Ask yourself:
   • Did I use God's name with respect?
   • Did I show my love for God and others in some way?
   • Did I usually say my daily prayers?
   • Did I always obey my mother and father?
   • Was I kind to those around me or was I mean?
   • Was I fair in the way that I played and worked with others?

   • Did I share my things with others?
   • Did I avoid taking what belongs to someone else?
   • Did I care for my own things and others' things?
   • Did I hurt others by calling them names or telling lies about them?
   • Did I go to Mass and take part in the celebration?

4. Pray for the Holy Spirit's help to change and follow Jesus' example of love.

Dear Candidate,

This is a very special time for you. You are preparing to take another step in your journey of friendship with Jesus and the Church. Your journey began when you were baptized. This journey of faith never ends. You will keep growing in your friendship with Jesus and the Church for your whole life.

In some parishes, young people celebrate the Sacrament of Confirmation before receiving Holy Communion for the first time. In other parishes, young people receive Holy Communion and then, when they are older, they celebrate the Sacrament of Confirmation.

What sacraments will you be celebrating this year?

_____

_____

During this time, you will

• learn about the Sacraments of Initiation

• pray with your friends and family

• listen to the stories of Jesus and the Apostles

• learn about the parts of the Mass

• prepare to celebrate the sacraments

What is your favorite part of the Mass?

_____

_____

What are you looking forward to learning this year?

_____

_____

My Faith Journey

I was baptized on _____ at _____.

My godparents are _____.

I was baptized by _____.

I was confirmed on _____ at _____.

My sponsor was _____.

I was confirmed by _____.

I celebrated Reconciliation
for the first time on _____

at _____.

I celebrated my First Communion on _____

at _____ .

_____ presided at the Eucharist.

Some of the people who helped me prepare for First Communion were

_____

_____

What I remember most about preparing for my First Communion

_____

_____

_____

What I remember most about my First Communion Day

_____

_____

7 We Belong

We Gather

Procession

As you sing, walk forward slowly. Follow the person carrying the Bible.

🎼 *Sing together.*

I believe in God the Father
I believe in God the Son
I believe in the Spirit
And the strength that makes
    us one
I believe that Mother Mary
Sits with Jesus at God's hand
I believe
I do believe.

© 2000 John Burland

Leader: Let us pray.

Make the Sign of the Cross together.

Ritual Focus: Renewal of Baptismal Promises

Leader: On the day of your Baptism, your family and the Church claimed you for Christ. You received the gifts of faith and new life. Today let us remember the promises of Baptism together.

Come forward and gather around the water and candle.

Leader: Do you say "no" to sin, so that you can live always as God's children?

All: I do.

Leader: Do you believe in God, the Father almighty?

All: I do.

Leader: Do you believe in Jesus Christ, his only Son, our Lord?

All: I do.

Leader:	Do you believe in the Holy Spirit, the holy catholic Church, the communion of saints?
All:	I do.
Leader:	This is our faith. This is the faith of the Church. We are proud to profess it in Jesus Christ.
All:	Amen.

BASED ON RITE OF BAPTISM FOR
CHILDREN, 144–146

Leader:	Let us come to the water and thank God for the gift of our Baptism.

One at a time, make the Sign of the Cross with the water.

Leader:	[Name], you are the light of Christ.
Candidate:	Amen.

We Listen

Leader:	God, our Father, open our hearts to the Holy Spirit as we remember our Baptism. We ask this through Jesus Christ our Lord.
All:	Amen.
Leader:	A reading from the holy Gospel according to John.
All:	Glory to you, Lord.
Leader:	*Read John 15:1–17.* The Gospel of the Lord.
All:	Praise to you, Lord Jesus Christ.

Sit silently.

We Go Forth

Leader:	Loving God, we thank you for the gift of Baptism. Send us forth to bring your love to others. We ask this through Jesus Christ our Lord.
All:	Amen.

🎼 *Sing the opening song together.*

New Life

SIGNS OF FAITH

Water

Water gives life. It cleans and makes things like new. The water used at Baptism is blessed. The blessed water is a sign that God the Father gives us his life and cleanses us from all sin. Through the waters of Baptism, we have new life in Jesus. Every time we go into a church, we make the sign of the cross with holy water. We remember our Baptism.

Reflect

Renewal of baptismal promises Imagine that an unbaptized friend was watching as you renewed your baptismal promises and sent you this e-mail message. Write a response to explain.

Hey, what were you doing in that ceremony? Heard you say "I do," "I do," "I do." What ARE you DO - ING?

_____

_____

_____

The Body of Christ

Baptism makes us children of God and members of the Church, the **Body of Christ**. At Baptism we are given new life with Jesus Christ. **Original sin** and all personal sins are forgiven. At Baptism we receive the light of Christ and become his followers. People who follow Jesus are called disciples. Another name for a follower of Christ is *Christian*.

Baptism makes us members of the Church. When we are baptized we belong to the Church and become special friends of God. We need Baptism to have life with God forever. In Baptism God the Holy Spirit comes to live in us.

The Holy Spirit:

- helps us believe and have faith

- shows us how to pray

- guides us to be the light of Christ for others and makes us holy

- helps us follow God's law

SIGNS OF FAITH

Paschal Candle

Sometimes this candle is called the Easter candle. Every year at the Easter Vigil, a new candle is lit from the Easter fire. The deacon or priest carries it through the darkness. He sings, "Light of Christ," and the people sing, "Thanks be to God." The candle is lit at all the Masses during the Easter season and at all Baptisms and funerals. During Baptisms the priest or deacon lights the candles for those being baptized from the **Paschal candle**.

We Belong to God

Faith Focus

What does Jesus tell us about belonging to God?

Jesus knew he would be returning to God, his Father. Jesus' disciples were sad. They wanted to stay close to him. Jesus wanted to tell his friends that he would always be with them. He wanted them to know that they belonged to him in a special way. So, he told them this story.

Scripture

JOHN 15:1–12

The Vine and the Branches

"I am the true vine, and my Father is the vine grower. He takes away every branch in me that does not bear fruit, and every one that does he prunes so that it bears more fruit. You are already pruned because of the word that I spoke to you. Remain in me as I remain in you. Just as a branch cannot bear fruit on its own unless it remains, so neither can you unless you remain in me. I am the vine. You are the branches. Whoever remains in me and I in him will bear much fruit because without me you can do nothing.

"As the Father loves me, so I also love you. Remain in my love. If you keep my commandments, you will remain in my love. This is my commandment: love one another as I love you. No one has greater love than this, to lay down one's life for one's friends. You are my friends if you do what I command you. I have told you everything I have heard from my Father. You did not choose me. I chose you and appointed you to go forth and bear fruit that will remain, so that whatever you ask the Father in my name he may give you. This I command you: love one another."

BASED ON JOHN 15:1–17

? **Name three things Jesus is telling his friends in this story.**

? **Describe your friendship with Jesus.**

Faith at Home

Read the scripture story with your family members. Answer the questions and discuss everyone's responses. Decide one action you can take as a family to strengthen your friendship with Jesus.

Share

Draw a picture With a partner think about and discuss other images, similar to the vine and branches, which could be used to show our connection to Jesus. Choose one of the images, and draw it on a large sheet of poster paper. Share your image with the whole group. Explain why it is similar to the vine and branches image.

The Sacraments of Initiation

SIGNS OF FAITH

The Holy Trinity

God the Father, God the Son, and God the Holy Spirit are the three Persons in one God. The three Persons act together in all they do, but each Person also has a special role. We sometimes call God the Father the Creator because he made everything. Jesus Christ is the Son of God and our Savior. God the Holy Spirit makes us holy. When we make the Sign of the Cross, we show our belief in the Trinity.

Faith Focus

Which sacraments are signs of belonging?

A sacrament is an effective sign that comes from Jesus and gives us grace, a share in God's life. Baptism, Confirmation, and Eucharist are called **Sacraments of Initiation**. We are joined closely to Christ and made full members of the Catholic Church through these sacraments. They are signs that we belong to God and to the Church.

Baptism

In Baptism the priest or deacon pours water over our head three times or lowers us into the water three times. As he does this he says, "I baptize you in the name of the Father, and of the Son, and of the Holy Spirit." Then he rubs blessed oil on our heads. This is called an anointing. In Baptism we receive the Holy Spirit. We may only be baptized once. As a sign of our new life in Christ, we receive a white garment. Then the priest or deacon gives our parent or godparent a lighted candle as a sign of faith. He prays that we will walk as children of the light and follow Jesus' example.

Confirmation

The Sacrament of **Confirmation** strengthens God's life in us. Confirmation completes our Baptism and helps us grow as followers of Jesus. In the sacrament, the bishop or priest puts his hand out and prays:

> "Send your Holy Spirit upon them to be their Helper and Guide."

Then the bishop or priest lays his hand on our heads and anoints us with the holy oil of **chrism**. Oil is a sign of strength. He says:

> "Be sealed with the Gift of the Holy Spirit."

These words tell us that we receive the Holy Spirit in a special way during Confirmation. Both Baptism and Confirmation mark us with a special character that shows we belong to Jesus forever.

Eucharist

The Sacrament of the **Eucharist** joins us in a very special way to Jesus. It is a sacred meal of thanksgiving in which Jesus shares his own Body and Blood with us in Holy Communion.

You already participate in the Eucharist by coming to Mass with your family.

❓ **In what ways are the Sacraments of Initiation signs of belonging?**

Faith at Home

Ask family members to share stories and pictures of your Baptism with you. Tell them about renewing your baptismal promises in the celebration. Show them your e-mail response on page 90. Invite family members to share anything they would add to your e-mail message.

Children of Light

Respond

Brainstorm choices   In a small group, brainstorm ways that young people can keep their baptismal promises and be children of the light. Jot down each of the ideas below. Choose one that you will promise to practice this week. Circle it.

_____

_____

_____

_____

_____

_____

_____

Closing Blessing

Gather and begin with the Sign of the Cross.

Leader: God, our Father, we praise and thank you for choosing us to be your children.

All: Amen.

Leader: Jesus, the Son, we praise and thank you for showing us how to live and love.

All: Amen.

Leader: Holy Spirit, giver of God's gifts, we praise and thank you for guiding us on our way.

All: Amen.

Sing together.

I believe in God the Father
I believe in God the Son
I believe in the Spirit
And the strength that makes
   us one
I believe that Mother Mary
Sits with Jesus at God's hand
I believe
I do believe.

Faith at Home

Faith Focus

- A sacrament is an effective sign that comes from Jesus and gives us grace.

- Baptism, Confirmation, and Eucharist are called Sacraments of Initiation.

- The Sacraments of Initiation make us full members of the Church.

Ritual Focus
Renewal of Baptismal Promises

The celebration focused on the renewal of baptismal promises. During the week, use the text on pages 88–89 with your family members and have them renew their baptismal promises with you.

Family Prayer

God our Father, thank you for making us your children. We believe in you and we belong to you. We ask you to keep us close to you. Show us how to love each other as you have loved us. Amen.

Act

Share Together Read John 15:1–17. Talk about what actions show we are friends of Jesus. Use a shoe box to create a "Friends of Jesus" box. Invite family members to look for examples of how others are acting as friends of Jesus. Have them write the examples on pieces of paper during the week and place them in the box. At the end of the week, read the slips of paper and share what you have learned.

Do Together Discuss what you and your family can do to help babies who are born into families that do not have money for food or clothing. Decide one thing you might do to help. (Suggestions: Buy baby food or diapers for a homeless shelter, or pray for these children at a specific time every day.)

Friends of Jesus

We Gather

Ritual Focus: Procession and Gloria

As you sing, walk forward slowly. Follow the person carrying the Bible.

🎼 *Sing together.*

Glory to God in the highest,
    and peace to his people
        on earth.
Glory to God in the highest,
    and peace to his people
        on earth.

Marty Haugen © 1987 GIA Publications

Leader: Let us pray.

Make the Sign of the Cross together.

God, our Loving Father, we praise you for your goodness and thank you for the gift of your Son Jesus. Send us your Holy Spirit to help us live as your children. We ask this through Jesus Christ our Lord.

All: Amen.

Leader: Every Sunday we come together as God's people to praise him and to give him thanks for everything. Today we do the same.

Come forward and gather around the holy water and candle.

Lord Jesus, you came to gather all people into your Father's kingdom.

All: We give you glory and thanks.

Leader: Lord Jesus, you came to bring us new life.

All:	We give you glory and thanks.
Leader:	Lord Jesus, you came to save us.
All:	We give you glory and thanks.
Leader:	Let us give thanks and praise.

 Sing the opening song together.

We Listen

Leader:	God, our Father, you alone are holy. You give us life and all good things. We ask you to help us be grateful children who always remember your glory. We ask this through Jesus Christ our Lord.
All:	Amen.
Leader:	A reading from the Acts of the Apostles.
	Read Acts 2:42–47.
	The word of the Lord.
All:	Thanks be to God.
	Sit silently.

We Go Forth

Leader:	God, the Holy Spirit, we praise you and thank you for your gifts. May we act in ways that show your gifts to others. We ask this through Jesus Christ our Lord.
All:	Amen.

 Sing the opening song together.

Gathered Together

CELEBRATE

SIGNS OF FAITH

Assembly

Many different people come together at Mass. Each person comes to praise and give thanks to God and to ask for his blessing. When we gather together to give God thanks and praise, we are an **assembly** of people who believe in Jesus. When the assembly gathers, the Holy Trinity is there.

Reflect

Procession and Gloria Write a rhyming poem about ways you gather with friends. Include ways you gather at church.

_____

_____

_____

_____

_____

_____

_____

_____

_____

_____

_____

We Come Together

Every time we gather as a group, we come together to pray. When we begin to form the **procession** for our celebration, we are gathering for prayer. **Prayer** is talking and listening to God. The procession gathers us as a community ready for prayer.

During the Mass, we pray in many different ways. When we stand, we pray a prayer of reverence. Prayers can be said. We can say the Lord Have Mercy. We can ask for God's help. Prayers can be sung. We can sing the Gloria in Mass. We pray in silence during the Mass, too. One time we do this is during the silence after the Gospel reading.

SIGNS OF FAITH

Procession

A procession is a group of people moving forward as part of a celebration. Processions at Mass remind us that we are walking forward with God and that God is walking with us. At Mass the priest and other ministers come into the church in a procession. People bring the gifts to the altar in a procession. We walk in a procession to receive Jesus in Holy Communion.

We Gather as God's People

Faith Focus

What is a community of faith?

The early followers of Jesus gathered often to pray and to remember him. They were like a family. Their faith in Jesus made them a community of faith.

Scripture

ACTS 2:42–47

The Early Christians

The early Christian community gathered together over and over again. They devoted themselves to the teaching of the Apostles and to the communal life, to the breaking of the bread and to prayers. Awe came upon everyone, and many wonders and signs were done through the Apostles. All who believed were together and had all things in common; they would sell their property and possessions and divide among all according to each one's need.

Every day they devoted themselves to meeting together in the temple area and to breaking bread in their homes. They ate their meals with exultation and sincerity of heart, praising God and enjoying favor with all the people. And every day the Lord added to their number those who were being saved.

BASED ON ACTS 2:42–47

❓ **What made the early Christians a community of faith?**

❓ **How is your church a community of faith?**

Read the scripture story with your family members. Answer the questions and discuss everyone's responses. Discuss how you as a family are a community of faith. Talk about the ways your family and parish take care of the needs of other Christians. Choose one activity to do together this week to show you are a community of faith.

Share

Prepare a pantomime In small groups, prepare a pantomime showing one aspect of how your parish acts as a community of faith. Act out the pantomime for the larger group.

The People Gather

SIGNS OF FAITH

Prayer and Singing

Singing is a way to pray. When we sing during Mass, we lift our minds, hearts, and voices to praise God in a special way. The whole assembly sings songs and hymns. Sometimes the choir sings and the assembly listens. The priest sometimes sings parts of the Mass.

Faith Focus

What happens when we gather as a community of faith?

Like the first Christians, we celebrate the Eucharist with a community, too. Our faith community is our Church family. During Mass we come together as the Body of Christ. Every Sunday or Saturday evening we gather with our parish community for the celebration of Mass.

Sunday is an important day for Christians because Jesus rose from the dead on Easter Sunday. It is so important that the Church requires us to participate in Sunday Mass.

We come together as an assembly
- to give God thanks and praise
- to listen to God's word
- to remember Jesus' death, Resurrection, and Ascension
- to share the Lord's Body and Blood
- to be sent forth to live as Jesus' followers

When we gather for Mass, we greet one another. We share our joy as we sing and pray.

Introductory Rites

The prayers and actions that begin the Mass are called the Introductory Rites. The Introductory Rites help us turn our hearts and minds to the great celebration of the Eucharist. The priest leads the assembly in the celebration of the Mass. Mass begins when he walks in procession to the altar. All of us in the assembly stand and sing.

The priest greets us. He often says, "The Lord be with you," or similar words. We answer, "And also with you." We know that God the Father, his Son Jesus, and the Holy Spirit are with us. We believe Jesus is present in every part of the Mass. Together we thank God for his goodness.

Faith at Home

Ask your family members how they would answer the question. Discuss their responses. Invite them to tell which of the songs sung during Mass are their favorites. Sing some of them together. If you have the *Songs of Celebration* CD for this program, spend some time listening to the songs.

? How do we show we are united as we gather for the Mass?

Give Praise and Thanks

Respond

Write a letter In the space below, write a letter to God. In the letter tell how you will give him praise and thanks during the week.

_____

_____

_____

_____

_____

_____

_____

_____

_____

_____

Closing Blessing

Gather and begin with the Sign of the Cross.

Leader: God, our Father, we praise and thank you for gathering us as your children. Send us your Holy Spirit to increase our faith and make our community strong. We ask this in the name of Jesus Christ our Lord.

All: Amen.

Leader: Go in peace to love and serve the Lord.

All: Thanks be to God.

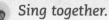 *Sing together.*

Glory to God in the highest,
  and peace to his people
    on earth.
Glory to God in the highest,
  and peace to his people
    on earth.

Marty Haugen © 1987 GIA Publications

Faith at Home

Faith Focus

- The Church is the People of God and the Body of Christ.

- The Eucharist, or Mass, is the Church's most important action of praise and thanks.

- The Introductory Rites gather us as a community of faith.

Ritual Focus
Procession and Gloria

The celebration focused on the Procession and Gloria. You sang the Gloria and prayed a litany of glory and praise to God. During the week, pray and talk about the meaning of the verses of the Gloria found on page 98.

Family Prayer

Loving God, we are your people. Thank you for the gift of faith. Help us to grow closer as a family. Strengthen our faith in you. Amen.

Act

Share Together Read Acts 2:42–47. Talk about what it must have been like for the early Christians to live as a community of faith. Emphasize the sharing of their possessions and their prayer life. With your family members, choose one way your family can continue to live as a community of faith, such as going to Mass or sharing your time and talent with others.

Do Together Together with your family members make a list of all the things you want to thank God for. Read the list as a litany. One person prays, "For sun and rain," and everyone responds, "We thank you, God." During the weeks ahead, select appropriate times to pray this thanksgiving prayer with your family or by yourself.

Litany

GO ONLINE **www.harcourtreligion.com**
Visit our Web site for weekly scripture readings and questions, family resources, and more activities.

9

We Are Forgiven

We Gather

Ritual Focus: Penitential Rite

🎵 *Sing together.*

Create in me a clean heart,
    O God.
A clean heart, O God,
    create in me.

© 1998, Tom Kendzia. Published by OCP

Leader: Let us pray.

Make the Sign of the Cross together.

Leader: Every week we come together as a community of faith. God wants us to be united with him and with one another as one family. Let us be quiet now and think about the times we have not been united to God or others.

Sit silently.

Leader: Let us pray for God's forgiveness and mercy.

Confiteor

Come forward, and gather around the holy water and candle.

All: I confess to almighty God, and to you, my brothers and sisters, that I have sinned through my own fault in my thoughts and in my words, in what I have done, and in what I have failed to do; and I ask blessed Mary, ever virgin, all the angels and saints, and you, my brothers and sisters, to pray for me to the Lord our God.

Leader: May God forgive us our sins and make us united with him and one another.

We Listen

Leader: God, our loving Father, you call us to forgiveness and peace. You want us to be united in you. We ask you to help us forgive others as you forgive us. We ask this through Jesus Christ our Lord.

All: Amen.

Leader: A reading from the holy Gospel according to Matthew.

All: Glory to you, Lord.

Leader: *Read Matthew 9:9–13.* The Gospel of the Lord.

All: Praise to you, Lord Jesus Christ.

Sit silently.

We Go Forth

Leader: Let us offer each other the Sign of Peace.

Give the Sign of Peace to one another.

Say: The Peace of the Lord be with you.

Answer: And also with you. Go forth united in God's love.

All: Amen.

Sing the opening song together.

God's Forgiveness

SIGNS OF FAITH

Lord Have Mercy

Sometimes in the Mass, during the Penitential Rite, we say the prayer, "Lord Have Mercy." These are the words that people say to Jesus when they ask him to heal them. When we pray these words at Mass, we ask Jesus to heal and forgive our sins and the sin of the world. We want everyone to be forgiven and united to God and one another forever.

Reflect

Confiteor In the celebration you prayed the Confiteor. With a partner, talk about what that prayer means to each of you. From your conversation develop three or four hand motions that could be used to express the meaning of the prayer as you pray it. Illustrate those hand motions and write the words that express what they mean next to the illustrations.

We Are One

Just like our parents want our families to be united, or joined together, God wants us to be united to him. He wants us to love and care for others, but we know that sometimes we do not show love to others and we are not always caring.

At the beginning of the Mass, we confess our sinfulness to God and one another in the Confiteor. When the assembly prays the Confiteor together, we are united in our sinfulness and in our need for God's forgiveness and mercy.

SIGNS OF FAITH

Silence

There are special times of quiet at Mass. These times of silence unite us to God. During the silent times we can listen or speak to God in our hearts. We keep our minds and hearts open to what God may be sharing with us.

Jesus Calls Sinners

Faith Focus
Why did Jesus eat with sinners?

Jesus made friends with people who had turned away from God. He ate and drank with them. He wanted them to know that God, his Father, welcomed them and wanted to be one with them.

Scripture

MATTHEW 9:9–13

The Call of Matthew

One day as Jesus was walking from town to town, he saw Matthew, a tax collector, sitting at the customs post. He said to him, "Follow me." And Matthew got up and followed him. While he was at the table in his house, many tax collectors and sinners came and sat with Jesus and his disciples.

The Pharisees, who were Jewish leaders and teachers, saw Jesus eating with sinners and tax collectors, and they said to Jesus' disciples, "Why does your teacher eat with tax collectors and sinners?" When Jesus heard their question, he said, "Those who are well do not need a physician, but the sick do. Go and learn the meaning of the words, 'I desire mercy, not sacrifice.' I did not come to call the righteous but sinners."

BASED ON MATHEW 9:9–13

❓ **Why did Jesus eat with sinners?**

❓ **How do you feel about Jesus eating with sinners?**

Faith at Home

Read the scripture story with your family members. Discuss situations where people in your family or school feel left out. Talk about ways you can reach out to them.

Share

Role-play   Gather in small groups or with a partner and describe a real-life situation that someone your age might face because he or she does not want to include someone who is disliked or looked down upon by others. Role-play a Christian response.

Penitential Rite

SIGNS OF FAITH

Sprinkling with Holy Water
During some Sunday Masses, the priest walks through the Church and sprinkles the assembly with holy water. The sprinkling reminds us of our Baptism. When the priest does the sprinkling with water, it takes the place of the Penitential Rite.

Faith Focus

What happens during the Penitential Rite?

Like the sinners in Jesus' time, sometimes we need Jesus to call us back to loving our Father:

- We may do things that hurt other people's feelings.

- We may fail to do things for people who need our help.

- We may not follow God's law and instead choose to do what we know is wrong.

When we do these things, we are not at one with God or others. When we come to Mass to share a meal with Jesus, Jesus welcomes us. It is a time to become one again with God and others. The Eucharist is a sacrament of forgiveness and unity. However, anyone who has not confessed mortal sins must first receive the Sacrament of Penance before going to Holy Communion.

We Are Sorry

After the opening song and greeting, we pray together for God's forgiveness during the Penitential Rite. We ask God to make us one again. The priest invites us to confess our sins to God and one another.

We pray the Confiteor, a prayer of sorrow that begins with the words "I confess." Sometimes we pray the Lord Have Mercy. When we do this, the priest prays three prayers to Jesus, and we answer him. We pray, "Lord have mercy, Christ have mercy, Lord have mercy." At the end of the Penitential Rite, the priest says this prayer:

"May almighty God have mercy on us, forgive us our sins, and bring us to everlasting life."

After the Penitential Rite, the Holy Spirit continues to unite us as an assembly. We are now ready to listen to God's word.

? **Why is the Penitential Rite important for the assembly?**

We Forgive

Respond

Make a bulletin board Display ways you forgive at home, school, or at church. Use words and drawings.

Closing Blessing

Gather and begin with the Sign of the Cross.

Leader: God, our Father, we praise and thank you for being a God who forgives.

All: Amen.

Leader: Jesus, our Savior, we praise and thank you for welcoming sinners and showing us how to live and love.

All: Amen.

Leader: Holy Spirit, giver of God's gifts, we praise and thank you for giving us courage to say I am sorry and to forgive others.

All: Amen.

♪ *Sing together.*

Create in me a clean heart, O God.
A clean heart, O God, create in me.

© 1998, Tom Kendzia. Published by OCP

Faith at Home

Faith Focus

- The Eucharist is a sacrament of unity and forgiveness.

- Sin keeps us from being one People of God.

- During the Penitential Rite we confess our sinfulness and ask God's forgiveness.

Ritual Focus
Penitential Rite

The celebration focused on the Penitential Rite. You prayed the Confiteor. This week at bedtime, pray the Confiteor before going to sleep.

Family Prayer

God of Mercy, thank you for always forgiving us. By the power of the Holy Spirit, help us to change and become more like your Son, Jesus. Make us one in love with you and all the people in our lives. Amen.

Act

Share Together Saying "I'm sorry" and "I forgive you" are important moments in the life of a family. Asking for and giving forgiveness can strengthen relationships. Sometimes we seek forgiveness in indirect ways by doing something special for the person we hurt. Have each family member draw a picture of one way they have seen a family member forgive another. Invite family members to share the story behind the picture.

Do Together Admitting we have hurt one another and saying "I am sorry" are not always easy things to do. Choose a time for family members to gather for prayer. Open with the prayer Come, Holy Spirit on page 191 of this book. Invite family members to ask for, give, and receive forgiveness for the times they may have hurt one another during the week.

GO ONLINE **www.harcourtreligion.com**
Visit our Web site for weekly scripture readings and questions, family resources, and more activities.

10 We Listen

We Gather

Procession

*As you sing, walk forward slowly.
Follow the person carrying
the Bible.*

🎼 *Sing together.*

Open my ears, Lord.
Help me to hear your voice.
Open my ears, Lord.
   Help me to hear.

© 1998, Jesse Manibusan.
Published by OCP Publications

Leader: Let us pray.

*Make the Sign of the
Cross together.*

We Listen

Leader: Father, send the Holy Spirit
to open our ears and hearts
that we may hear and live
your word. We ask this in
Jesus' name.

All: Amen.

Leader: A reading from the holy Gospel
according to Matthew.

All: Glory to you, Lord.

Ritual Focus: Signing

Leader: Loving Father, we want to live
by your word. May your word
be in our minds.

*Trace the Sign of the
Cross on your forehead.*

Leader: May your word be on our lips.

Trace the Sign of the Cross on your lips.

Leader: May your word be in our hearts.

Trace the Sign of the Cross on your heart.

Leader: We ask this through Jesus Christ our Lord.

All: Amen.

Leader: *Read Matthew 13:1–23.* The Gospel of the Lord.

All: Praise to you, Lord Jesus Christ.

Sit silently.

We Go Forth

Leader: Loving God, we thank you for your word. Help us remember and share it. We ask this through Jesus Christ our Lord.

All: Amen.

🎼 *Sing the opening song together.*

God's Word

SIGNS OF FAITH

The Sign of the Cross
Each of us is signed with the Sign of the Cross at our Baptism. The Sign of the Cross marks us as followers of Jesus. Every time we sign ourselves with the Sign of the Cross, we remember our Baptism. In Baptism we are called to be disciples who follow God's word.

Reflect

Signing   In the celebration, you traced the Sign of the Cross on your forehead, lips, and heart. You prayed that God's word would be in your mind, on your lips, and in your heart. Write a paragraph explaining what this means for you.

The Bible

We know that the **Bible** is God's own word. Another name for the Bible is Scriptures. *Scripture* means "writings." God inspired humans to write stories of his love and friendship. At Mass we listen to and remember those stories. The good news of the Sacred criptures is the same good news that Jesus taught.

God the Father, Jesus his Son, and the Holy Spirit are with us when we pray for God's word to be in our minds, on our lips, and in our hearts. They help us hear the good news and share it with others.

SIGNS OF FAITH

The Bible

The Bible has two parts. The parts of the Bible are the Old Testament and the New Testament. The Old Testament tells stories of the friendship between God and his people before the birth of Jesus. The New Testament tells the stories of Jesus and the people in the early Church.

Hear God's Word

Faith Focus

Why do we listen to God's word?

Jesus was a storyteller, and he told many stories about God. We find his stories in the Gospels. The word *gospel* means "good news." Many of Jesus' stories are parables, which are short stories that make a point and help us think about our relationship with God. They help us listen to and understand Jesus' message of good news.

One day Jesus told a parable about a sower. A sower is a person who puts seeds on the ground so they can grow.

Scripture

MATTHEW 13:1–23

The Sower

"A sower went out to sow. And as he sowed, some seed fell on the path, and birds came and ate it up. Some fell on rocky ground, where it had little soil. It sprang up at once because the soil was not deep, and when the sun rose it was scorched, and it withered for lack of roots. Some seed fell among thorns, and the thorns grew up and choked it. But some seed fell on rich soil, and produced fruit, a hundred or sixty or thirtyfold. Whoever has ears ought to hear."

The disciples approached him and said, "Why do you speak to them in parables?" Jesus answered, "because they look but do not see and hear but do not listen or understand."

Jesus went on to explain the story. He said, "Hear then the parable of the sower. The seed sown on the path is the one who hears the word of the kingdom without understanding it, and the evil one comes and steals away what was sown in his heart. The seed sown on rocky ground is the one who hears the word and receives it at once with joy. But he has no root and lasts only for a time. When some tribulation or persecution comes because of the word, he immediately falls away. The seed sown among thorns is the one who hears the word, but then worldly anxiety and the lure of riches choke the word and it bears no fruit. But the seed sown on rich soil is the one who hears the word and understands it, who indeed bears fruit and yields a hundred or sixty or thirtyfold."

BASED ON MATTHEW 13:1–23

❓ **Which of Jesus' descriptions applies to young people today?**

❓ **What steps can you take to hear and understand God's word?**

Faith at Home

Read the scripture story with your family members. Answer the questions, and discuss everyone's responses. Discuss the examples Jesus gives and how they relate to each of you. Decide one way your family can help each other listen to God's word and follow it.

Share

Write a modern-day story In small groups, choose one of the people Jesus was talking about in the parable. Make up a modern-day story of what might happen to that person when the "seed" falls on them.

The Liturgy of the Word

SIGNS OF FAITH

The Readings

The readings are read from a place called the **ambo**. The reader reads the first and second readings from a special book called the **lectionary**. The lectionary has all the Bible readings for every Sunday in it. The Gospel is read from the **Book of the Gospels**, which is carried in procession during the Introductory Rites to show the importance of the four Gospels.

Faith Focus

What happens during the Liturgy of the Word?

The Mass has two very important parts. The first part is the Liturgy of the Word. The second part is the Liturgy of the Eucharist. In the Liturgy of the Word, we feast on Jesus' presence in the word. In the Liturgy of the Eucharist, we feast on Jesus' presence in his Body and Blood.

During the Liturgy of the Word, we listen to three readings from the Bible. The first reading is usually from the Old Testament. The second reading is from the New Testament and tells more about the story of the early followers of Jesus. Between the first two readings, we sing or pray a psalm from the Old Testament. The psalm is a response, or answer, to God's word. It is called the Responsorial Psalm.

Gospel

The third reading always comes from one of the four Gospels. Each Gospel tells the story of the life, death, and Resurrection of Jesus. They are the heart of the Scriptures because they tell the good news of Jesus.

During the Mass we stand and greet the Gospel reading with joy. Most Sundays, except during Lent, we say or sing "Alleluia," which means "Praise the Lord." Sometimes the priest or deacon will incense the Book of the Gospels before the Gospel is proclaimed.

Our Response

After the readings the priest or deacon gives a homily to help us understand and follow God's word we have just heard. There is a period of silence after the homily when we think about how to live the word in our lives.

We respond to God's word when we stand and pray the Creed. In the Creed we proudly profess what we believe about the Trinity and the Church. Feasting on God's word makes us want to share with others who are hungry for good news. We close the Liturgy of the Word by praying together for the needs of the Church and for all people around the world. These special prayers are called the general intercessions or prayer of the faithful. The Creed and the general intercessions are our response to hearing God's word.

Faith at Home

Before going to Mass this weekend, remind family members to listen carefully to the readings and homily. Spend some time after Mass discussing how the readings or the homily relates to your family life.

❓ **What do we call the part of the Mass when we listen to God's word?**

Share God's Word

Respond

Make a poster Using newspapers and magazines, cut out stories and pictures that show God's word alive today in people and events. Paste the pictures on poster board. Choose one of the stories or pictures, and tell why you chose it. Describe how you are going to do something similar this week to show that God's word is alive in your own life.

Closing Blessing

Gather and begin with the Sign of the Cross.

Leader: We praise and thank you, Lord, for the gift of your word.

All: Alleluia.

Leader: Help us to go forth and listen for your word in all we do. Show us how to speak your good news to others.

All: Amen.

🎼 *Sing together.*

Open my ears, Lord.
Help me to hear your voice.
Open my ears, Lord.
Help me to hear.

© 1998, Jesse Manibusan.
Published by OCP Publications

Faith at Home

Faith Focus

- The Bible is God's word written in human words.

- We listen to the word of God during the Liturgy of the Word.

- When we listen to God's word, we want to share it with others.

Ritual Focus
Signing

The celebration focused on Signing and listening to God's word. You prayed by signing yourself with the Sign of the Cross on your forehead, lips, and heart before the Gospel was proclaimed. You prayed that God's word would be with you. At appropriate times during the week, pray the signing prayer on pages 118–119 with your family.

Family Prayer

Jesus, bless us as we listen for your word this week. Open our eyes, our hearts, and our minds that we will become more faithful followers and have the courage to spread your word to all those we meet. Amen.

Act

Share Together Have your family members name people in your neighborhood or the world who are in need of seeing God's word alive today. Create a family prayer of the faithful, and pray it this week during times you are together.

Do Together Read Matthew 13:1–23, and talk about the question, "How can we bring the word of God to someone in need this week?" Check in your parish bulletin for the names of those who might appreciate a get-well card or a card of encouragement. Have family members include their favorite verses in the card.

Mom
Dad
Sheila
Aunt Kathy
Uncle Bill

GO ONLINE **www.harcourtreligion.com**
Visit our Web site for weekly scripture readings and questions, family resources, and more activities.

11

We Prepare

We Gather

Procession

As you sing, walk forward slowly. Follow the person carrying the Bible.

🎼 *Sing together.*

We praise you, O Lord
For all your works are
    wonderful.
We praise you, O Lord
Forever is your love.

© 1978, Damean Music.
Distributed by GIA Publications

Leader: Let us pray.

Make the Sign of the Cross together.

Ritual Focus: Honoring the Cross

Leader: God gives us many gifts. He gives us sun and rain. He gives us family and friends. He gives us our life. The most important gift God gives us is his Son, Jesus. Jesus shows us how to live. When Jesus died on the cross, he gave his life for all people. Let us think about what a wonderful gift Jesus gave us.

Sit silently.

Come forward, and put your hand on the cross.

We Listen

Leader: Gracious God, open our hearts to hear your word. We ask this through Jesus Christ our Lord.

All: Amen.

Leader: A reading from the holy Gospel according to John.

All: Glory to you, Lord.

Trace the Sign of the Cross on your forehead, lips, and heart.

Leader: Read John 13:4–16.

The Gospel of the Lord.

All: Praise to you, Lord Jesus Christ.

Sit silently.

Leader: Lord God, send us the Holy Spirit to show us how to live for others. We ask this in the name of Jesus, your Son.

All: Amen.

Leader: Let us pray as Jesus taught us:

Pray the Lord's Prayer together.

Let us offer each other the Sign of Peace.

Offer one another a sign of Christ's peace.

Say: The Peace of the Lord be with you.

Answer: And also with you.

We Go Forth

Leader: Loving God, send us out to share our lives with others. We ask this through Jesus Christ our Lord.

All: Amen.

 Sing the opening song together.

The Cross

SIGNS OF FAITH

The Cross

The cross reminds us that Jesus gave his life for us. We see the cross in the church near the altar. On most Sundays the cross is carried in the Entrance Procession. On Good Friday we honor the cross in a special service. When a cross has a figure of Jesus on it, it is called a crucifix.

Reflect

Honoring the cross Think back to the celebration. Recall placing your hand on the cross or crucifix and watching others in your group do the same. In the space below, express in words, phrases, or poetry your thoughts and feelings about the cross, your relationship to Jesus, or the Church.

_____

_____

_____

_____

_____

_____

_____

_____

_____

_____

Sacrifice

The cross reminds us that Jesus died for us. He died for our sins. He gave up his life as a **sacrifice** for all people. *Sacrifice* means "giving up something out of love for someone else." What a wonderful gift Jesus gave us—his life.

We sacrifice when we share with others or when we give up something valuable such as time, possessions, or money to help another person. Usually we make sacrifices for those we love and care for.

When the Church gathers for Mass, we remember the sacrifice of Jesus on the cross. He gave up his life to save us. The Mass is our sacrifice, too. At Mass we also remember what we have done for God and others. We offer God the gift of our lives.

SIGNS OF FAITH

The Altar

The **altar** is the central table in the front of the church. It is a sign of Jesus' presence with us. It is also a sign that the Mass is a sacrifice and a meal. From ancient times altars were the place where sacrifices were offered. In the Christian tradition, another name for the altar is "the Table of the Lord."

We Serve Others

Faith Focus
What does Jesus tell us about serving others?

On the night before he died, Jesus was at supper with his friends. He wanted to show his friends how much he loved them. He wanted to teach them how to show God's love to others.

Scripture

JOHN 13:4–16

The Washing of the Feet

While Jesus was at the Last Supper with his disciples, he rose from the table. He took a towel and tied it around his waist. Then he poured water into a basin and began to wash the disciples' feet. He came to Simon Peter who said to him, "Master, are you going to wash my feet?" Jesus answered and said to him, "What I am doing you do not understand now, but you will understand later."

Peter said to him, "You will never wash my feet." Jesus answered him, "Unless I wash you, you will have no inheritance with me." Simon Peter said to him, "Master, then not only my feet but my hands and head as well." Then Jesus washed the feet of all the disciples.

When he was finished, Jesus said, "Do you understand what I just did? You call me 'teacher' and 'master.' And you are right, I am. If I have washed your feet, then you should wash one another's feet. I have given you a model to follow. What I do for you, you should do for others."

BASED ON JOHN 13:4–16

? **Why do you think Jesus washed the disciples' feet?**

? **What does Jesus want you to do for others?**

Faith at Home

Read the scripture story with family members. Discuss your responses to both questions. Ask family members to share times they have seen others give up or do something out of love for others.

Share

Write a story On a separate sheet of paper, write a story about a young person about your age who lives in your town, who makes a sacrifice for a friend. Be sure to describe how and why the young person decided to make that choice.

The Sacrifice of the Mass

SIGNS OF FAITH

Bread and Wine

Bread and wine are foods that people use for special meals. At Mass we use bread that is made without yeast. The wine comes from grapes. By the power of the Holy Spirit and the words and action of the priest, the bread and wine become the Body and Blood of Jesus. They become our spiritual food.

Faith Focus

What gifts do we bring to the altar?

When Jesus washed the feet of the disciples, he showed us a model of how we are called to give our lives for others in service. Jesus gave his life for us on the cross. He saved us from our sins by his life, death, and Resurrection.

The Liturgy of the Eucharist is the second main part of the Mass. *Eucharist* means "thanksgiving." During the Liturgy of the Eucharist we recall and make present Jesus' sacrifice. Through the power of the Holy Spirit and the action of the priest, Jesus offers again the gift of himself to his Father.

During the Liturgy of the Eucharist, we thank God the Father for Jesus' sacrifice on the cross and we bring our own lives and our sacrifices to the altar.

The sacrifices we make during the week are our gifts to God. They prepare us to join in Jesus' sacrifice.

Preparation of the Altar and the Gifts

The Liturgy of the Eucharist begins with the Preparation of the Altar and the Gifts. Members of the assembly bring the bread and wine to the priest, and they are placed on the altar.

We also offer gifts of money or other gifts for the poor and needy. This offering is called a **collection**. These offerings help the parish do its work and take care of those in need. The money offering is also a sign of our sacrifice.

The priest prepares the bread and wine and gives God thanks for his goodness.

We answer, "Blessed be God for ever."

Then the priest prays that our sacrifice will be acceptable to God.

We answer, "May the Lord accept the sacrifice at your hands for the praise and glory of his name, for our good, and the good of all his Church."

Faith at Home

Talk with family members about what gifts each of you brings to Mass. Discuss ways you can contribute your time, talent, or money as a gift to God. Use this page to review the responses for the Preparation of the Altar and the Gifts.

❓ **What gifts do you bring to Mass?**

I Serve Others

Respond

Make a poster calendar   Using magazines and newspapers, select pictures and stories that show people serving others and making sacrifices. Paste them onto a poster board. At the bottom of the poster, design a seven-day calendar with seven writing spaces. Every day this week, record one service or sacrifice you were able to make for others.

Closing Blessing

Gather and begin with the Sign of the Cross.

Leader: God, our Father, we praise and thank you for the gift of your Son, Jesus.

All: Amen.

Leader: Jesus, our Savior, we praise and thank you for giving up your life for us.

All: Amen.

Leader: Holy Spirit, giver of God's gifts, we praise and thank you for being with us. Show us how to care about others.

All: Amen.

Sing together.

We praise you, O Lord
For all your works are
  wonderful.
We praise you, O Lord
Forever is your love.

Faith at Home

Faith Focus

- Jesus sacrificed his life for us when he died on the cross.

- The Mass is a sacrifice.

- At Mass through the power of the Holy Spirit and the words and actions of the priest, Jesus offers again the gift of himself to his Father and to us.

Ritual Focus
Honoring the Cross

The celebration focused on Honoring the Cross. You honored the cross during the celebration. Obtain a cross or crucifix, and place it where you will be reminded of Jesus' gift of his life for us. When you see it, pray a prayer of thanks.

Family Prayer

Gracious God, thank you for the gift of each other and especially for the gift of Jesus. Help us remain in your love and teach us to share it with others. Amen.

Act

Share Together Read John 13:4–16. With your family members, talk about what Jesus meant when he said, "What I do for you, you should do for others." Together make a list of people who serve your family, such as sanitation workers, street crossing guards, doctors, and dentists. Discuss ways your family can thank these people for sharing their gifts. Choose one of them and act on it.

Do Together With your family members, name some neighbors, family members, or friends who are in need of help or companionship, such as someone who is sick, lives alone, or needs to be tutored. Make a list of actions your family can take to serve these people sometime in the next month. Decide who will do what, and then mark it on the calendar.

CELEBRATE

We Gather

Procession

As you sing, walk forward slowly. Follow the person carrying the Bible.

🎵 *Sing together.*

Te alabaré, Señor;
   tú me has librado.
I will praise you Lord;
   you have rescued me.

Tony Alonso © 2003 GIA Publications

Leader: Let us pray.

Make the Sign of the Cross together.

We Listen

Leader: Loving Father, we come before you to remember and give thanks for what your Son, Jesus, did for us. Open our hearts to the Holy Spirit that we will understand your word. We ask this through Jesus Christ our Lord.

All: Amen.

Leader: A reading from the holy Gospel according to Luke.

All: Glory to you, Lord.

Trace the Sign of the Cross on your forehead, lips, and heart.

Leader: Read Luke 22:14–20.

The Gospel of the Lord.

All: Praise to you, Lord Jesus Christ.

Sit silently.

Ritual Focus: Memorial Acclamation

Leader: Every time we gather together at the Eucharist, we know Jesus comes again to be with us. We are happy. We give God the Father thanks and praise for the mystery of Jesus' presence. We pray.

Kneel.

Let us proclaim the mystery of faith:

All: Christ has died.
Christ is risen.
Christ will come again.

Stand.

Leader: Let us pray as Jesus taught us:

Pray the Lord's Prayer together.

Leader: Let us offer each other the Sign of Peace.

Offer one another a sign of Christ's peace.

Say: The Peace of the Lord be with you.

Answer: And also with you.

We Go Forth

Leader: Loving Father, send us forth to bring Jesus' presence to one another. Help us to remember him. We ask this through Jesus Christ our Lord.

All: Amen.

 Sing together.

We Remember

SIGNS OF FAITH

Kneeling

We kneel as a sign that we are God's children. When we kneel, we show we depend on God. Kneeling is one of the many ways we use our bodies to pray. Sometimes we kneel when we want to ask God for something. Other times we kneel when we seek God's forgiveness. At Mass we kneel after the Holy, Holy, Holy through the Great Amen. We also kneel during the Lamb of God before Holy Communion.

Reflect

Memorial Acclamation Think and write about the celebration.

When I heard the story of the Last Supper

_____

_____

_____

When I knelt down

_____

_____

_____

Write a short paragraph and explain why the words, "Christ has died, Christ is risen, Christ will come again" are important for you.

_____

_____

_____

_____

_____

_____

The Eucharistic Prayer

The Eucharistic Prayer is the Church's great prayer of praise and thanksgiving to God. The priest begins this prayer, and then we sing with all the angels and saints, "Holy, Holy, Holy." Then we kneel as the prayer continues.

The priest prays the epiclesis, a prayer that God will send the Holy Spirit to make our gifts holy so they become the Body and Blood of Jesus. He retells the story of the Last Supper and we remember what Jesus did for us on the night before he died.

We proclaim the **mystery** of our faith. A mystery of faith is something we believe but we do not understand. We believe that Jesus is with us now and we believe that all people who love God will live with him in heaven when they die. We believe because Jesus promised us that this is true. We want to say, "thank you" for this wonderful mystery.

Jesus Gives Thanks

Faith Focus

What does Jesus tell his friends?

Long ago, God led the people of Israel out of the land of Egypt where they had been slaves. He saved the people and set them free. Every year at the Passover meal, Jewish people remember and give thanks for God's saving love. They remember God's promises.

Scripture

MATTHEW 26:26–28 AND LUKE 22:14–20

The Last Supper

On the night before he died, Jesus shared a special meal with his Apostles. They gathered to celebrate the Passover, a great Jewish holiday of thanksgiving.

We call this meal the Last Supper. During the meal, Jesus told his followers how to remember the mystery of our faith.

When it was time to begin, Jesus told his disciples that he had looked forward to eating the Passover meal with them. He said, "I have eagerly desired to eat this Passover with you before I suffer."

Jesus then used the bread and wine of the Passover in a new way. While they were eating, Jesus took bread, said the blessing, and broke it. He gave it to his disciples and said, "Take and eat, this is my body."

Then Jesus took a cup of wine, gave thanks, and gave it to them, saying "Drink from it all of you, for this is the blood of the covenant, which will be shed for many for the forgiveness of sins. Do this in memory of me."

BASED ON MATTHEW 26:26–28 AND LUKE 22:14–20

? **What did Jesus and his disciples remember at the Passover?**

? **How do you remember Jesus?**

Faith at Home

Read the scripture story with your family members and discuss their responses to the questions. Talk about ways your family remembers important events, such as patriotic holidays, birthdays, and anniversaries.

Share

Create a parish bulletin announcement With a partner, create a four- or five-line parish bulletin announcement on a separate piece of paper. Title the announcement, "Do this in memory of me."

We Remember and Give Thanks

SIGNS OF FAITH

Blessed Sacrament

The consecrated Bread and Wine are the Body and Blood of Jesus. They are called the Blessed Sacrament. After Mass the remaining Hosts are put in a special place called a **tabernacle**. The tabernacle is usually in a chapel or at a side altar in the church. We keep the Blessed Sacrament there so it can be brought to parish members who are ill and cannot be present. We can also spend time before the tabernacle praying to Jesus in the Blessed Sacrament.

Faith Focus

What do we remember and give thanks for during the Eucharistic Prayer?

Another name for the Eucharist is "The Lord's Supper." At the Last Supper Jesus and the disciples remembered the Passover. As they remembered the story, they said special prayers of thanks. At Mass we remember the Last Supper and Jesus' death on the cross; we too, say special prayers of thanks.

During the Eucharistic Prayer, the priest joins all of our prayers into one. He prays in our name and the name of the Church. We take part in the prayer, too. During the prayer we remember all the ways that God has saved us. We offer ourselves to God with Jesus. We share in Jesus' death and Resurrection through the power of the Holy Spirit. We remember and we say "thank you" for:

- all of God's gifts
- the gift of Jesus, God's Son
- Jesus' death, his Resurrection, and his Ascension
- Jesus' promise

The priest asks God to accept our sacrifice. We pray that God will make us holy like the saints in heaven with him. We pray for one another. We offer the Mass for the people who have died.

Consecration

An important part of the Eucharistic Prayer is the **consecration**. The priest says the words Jesus did at the Last Supper. The gifts of bread and wine become the Body and Blood of Christ. Through the power of the Holy Spirit and the words and actions of the priest, Jesus becomes really, truly, present in the bread and wine.

Only an ordained priest can consecrate the gifts of bread and wine. After the consecration we remember that Jesus gave his life for us. The priest says or sings: "Let us proclaim the mystery of faith." We answer with a special response: "Christ has died, Christ is risen, Christ will come again." This response is called the Memorial Acclamation.

The Great Amen

At the end of the Eucharistic Prayer, the priest prays the prayer that begins,

"Through him, with him, and in him. . ."

We answer, "Amen."

This is the Great Amen. When we pray the Great Amen, we say "yes" to God's promises. We praise him for his gifts and saving actions.

❓ **How is the Eucharist like the Last Supper?**

Faith at Home

Explain your response to the question with your family members. If you have friends who are Jewish, ask if you can invite them to your home to share a meal and talk about what Passover means to them.

145

Say "Yes"

Respond

Create an amen list   When we say "Amen" at the end of the Eucharistic Prayer, we are saying "yes" to God's promises—not just at Mass, but also in our daily life. In the space below, make a list of ways that you show your belief in Jesus and say "Amen" every day.

"My Amen List"

Closing Blessing

Gather and begin with the Sign of the Cross.

Leader: God, our Father, we remember and give thanks for all your good gifts.

All: Amen.

Leader: Jesus, our Savior, we remember and give thanks for your death and Resurrection.

All: Amen.

Leader: Holy Spirit, we remember and give thanks that you are with us.

All: Amen.

 Sing together.

Te alabaré, Señor;
  tú me has librado.
I will praise you Lord;
  you have rescued me.

Tony Alonso © 2003 GIA Publications

Faith at Home

Faith Focus

- The Eucharistic Prayer is a prayer of thanksgiving, remembering, and consecration.

- Through the power of the Holy Spirit and the words and actions of the priest, the bread and wine become the Body and Blood of Jesus.

- At the Great Amen, the assembly says "yes" to all of God's saving actions and promises.

Ritual Focus
Memorial Acclamation

The celebration focused on the Memorial Acclamation. You prayed an Acclamation. During the week, use the Family Prayer as a prayer before or after meals.

Family Prayer

Giving God, we give you thanks for all the gifts you give us: for the gifts of creation, for family and friends, and especially for the gift of your Son, Jesus. Help us to always remember that you are here with us. Amen.

Act

Share Together Talk about ways your family remembers people who have moved away or died. Use examples of pictures or stories to get the sharing started. Make a list of the examples that family members share. Use the list to talk about ways your family can remember Jesus during the week.

Do Together Invite family members to plan a time to make a visit to the Blessed Sacrament together. Your parish church may have a Blessed Sacrament chapel in the church, or the tabernacle may be in another special place. Go near the place where the tabernacle is located. Spend some quiet time in conversation with Jesus in the Blessed Sacrament.

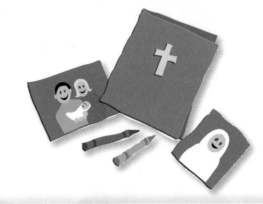

GO ONLINE **www.harcourtreligion.com**
Visit our Web site for weekly scripture readings and questions, family resources, and more activities.

13

We Share a Meal

CELEBRATE

We Gather

Procession

As you sing, walk forward slowly. Follow the person carrying the Bible.

🎵 *Sing together.*

We come to the Table of
   the Lord
As one body formed in
   your love.
We come to the Table of
   the Lord
As one body formed in
   your love.

© 2005 John Burland

Leader: Let us pray.

Make the Sign of the Cross together.

We Listen

Leader: God, our Father, you provide us with everything we need. Strengthen us to bring life to others. We ask this through Jesus Christ our Lord.

All: Amen.

Leader: A reading from the holy Gospel according to John.

All: Glory to you, Lord.

Trace the Sign of the Cross on your forehead, lips, and heart.

Leader: *Read John 6:30–58.*

The Gospel of the Lord.

All: Praise to you, Lord Jesus Christ.

Sit silently.

Ritual Focus: Sharing a Meal

Be seated around the table.

Leader: Blessed are you,
almighty Father,

who gives us our
daily bread.

Blessed is your only
begotten Son,

who continually feeds us
with the word of life.

Blessed is the Holy Spirit,

who brings us together at
this table of love.

Blessed be God now and
for ever.

All: Amen.

BOOK OF BLESSINGS, 1069

Share the food at the table.

Leader: We give you thanks for
all your gifts, almighty
God, living and reigning
now and forever.

All: Amen.

BOOK OF BLESSINGS, 1070

We Go Forth

Leader: Loving God, we thank you for
food, for families, for friends,
and for the gift of your Son,
Jesus. Help us to share the gifts
of life with others. We ask this in
the name of your Son, Jesus.

All: Amen.

 Sing the opening song together.

Special Meals

Sign of Peace

SIGNS OF FAITH

During Mass we offer one another the **Sign of Peace** before Holy Communion. The Sign of Peace is an action prayer. We reach out our hands to people around us. We wish them God's peace. Giving the Sign of Peace to others is a sign that we are united with one another at the Table of the Lord.

Reflect

Sharing a meal   Fill out the following questionnaire about sharing a meal.

1.   What is your favorite meal?

_____

2.   What do you like best about eating with other people?

_____

3.   What do you like least about eating with other people?

_____

4.   In your family, what is the difference between an ordinary meal and a special meal?

_____

5.   What are your family rules about mealtime?

_____

6.   Who blesses the meal when you are together?

_____

The Eucharist as a Meal

Sharing a meal brings people closer together. A special meal, sometimes called a banquet or feast, is a time to celebrate. It is a time to share stories, sing songs, and eat special food. When families and friends gather for special meals, they grow in love.

The Eucharist is the Church's special meal. The Holy Spirit gathers us with our parish family and with Catholics all over the world. We gather at the Eucharist as the Body of Christ to celebrate God's love for us. We also share Jesus' own Body and Blood in Holy Communion. Jesus is truly present in both the consecrated Bread and the Wine.

Jesus is the Bread of Life. In the meal of the Eucharist, we share in the life of the Risen Christ.

We Share the Bread of Life

Faith Focus

What does Jesus tell us about himself?

Jesus shared many meals with people. One time, a crowd followed Jesus up a hill. They had not had much to eat. Jesus saw that they were hungry, and he fed them with only five loaves of bread and a few fish. The people were amazed!

Scripture

JOHN 6:30–58

I Am the Bread of Life

When the people saw Jesus feed so many with so little food, they wanted to do the works of God. So they said to him, "What can we do to accomplish the works of God?" Jesus answered, "This is the work of God, that you believe in me." So they said to him, "What sign can you do that we may see and believe in you? What can you do?" They said, "When Moses and the people of Israel were hungry in the dessert, Moses gave them manna, bread from heaven." But Jesus reminded them that it was God the Father, not Moses, who gave food to the people. Then he taught the people a very important lesson about himself.

"My Father sent me to bring you life that lasts forever. I myself am the bread of life; whoever comes to me will never be hungry. No one who believes in me will ever be thirsty."

Jesus continued, "I am the bread from heaven. The people who ate manna in the desert eventually died, as all humans die. But if you share my own flesh and blood, I will always be with you. You will live forever with God."

"What is he talking about?" some people asked. Jesus answered them, "I am the bread of life. Whoever eats it will live forever. Just as the Father sent me and I have life because of him, so too will the one who eats the bread of life live forever."

BASED ON JOHN 6:30–58

❓ **What do you think Jesus means when he says he is the Bread of Life?**

❓ **How can you share in Jesus' life?**

Faith at Home

Read the scripture story with your family. Talk about the connections between the effects of food for our physical bodies and Jesus as the food for our spirit. Together, decide on one activity you can do this week to remember that Jesus is the Bread of Life.

Share

Sketch a design In small groups or with a partner, sketch a billboard design on a separate piece of paper that shows members of your group inviting other people to share in Jesus' life. Give your design an interesting title.

The Communion Rite

Lamb of God

The **Lamb of God** is a title for Jesus. This title reminds us that Jesus gave his life for our sins. When we pray or sing this prayer before Holy Communion, we remember that through Jesus' death and Resurrection, our sins are forgiven and we have peace.

Faith Focus

What happens during the Communion Rite?

We receive Jesus, the Bread of Life, in Holy Communion. What does this mean?

- We are united with Jesus.

- Our friendship with Jesus grows stronger.

- God forgives our less serious sins if we are sorry and gives us strength to avoid serious sin.

- We are united with the whole Church, the Body of Christ.

- We share in God's promise that we will live in heaven with Jesus, Mary, and all the saints.

We prepare ourselves to receive Holy Communion. Together we stand and pray the Lord's Prayer. We remember we are one family with God. As a sign of unity, we share the Sign of Peace with each other.

Holy Communion

When the time comes for Holy Communion, the priest invites us to the table. He reminds us of Jesus' sacrifice and presence in the Eucharist. He holds up the large Host and says, "This is the Lamb of God, who takes away the sin of the world. Happy are we who are called to his supper." We come forward in a procession. Sometimes we sing a song.

When it is our turn to receive Jesus, we cup our hands with one hand on top of the other. The priest, deacon, or extraordinary minister of Holy Communion says, "The Body of Christ." We answer, "Amen."

We often receive from the cup. After we swallow the Host, we go to the deacon or extraordinary minister of Holy Communion, who offers the cup. We hear, "The Blood of Christ." We answer, "Amen." We return to our places. We pray or sing a prayer of thanksgiving.

We should receive Holy Communion every time we participate in the Mass. We must do so at least once a year.

❓ **Why are we happy to share in the Lord's Supper?**

Faith at Home

Ask family members to share their responses to the question. Talk about what happens when we receive Holy Communion by referring to the list on page 154. Together look at the pictures on pages 154 and 155, and review how to go to Holy Communion.

Receive Jesus

Respond

Write a prayer In the space below, write a prayer. Share your thoughts and feelings about participating fully in the Mass by receiving Jesus in Holy Communion.

_____

_____

_____

_____

_____

_____

_____

Closing Blessing

Gather and begin with the Sign of the Cross.

Leader: God, our Father, we praise and thank you for the gift of life.

All: Amen.

Leader: Jesus, our Savior, we praise and thank you for giving yourself to us in Holy Communion.

All: Amen.

Leader: Holy Spirit, giver of God's gifts, we praise and thank you for helping us live as members of the Body of Christ.

All: Amen.

🎼 *Sing together.*

We come to the Table of the Lord
As one body formed in your love.
We come to the Table of the Lord
As one body formed in your love.

© 2005 John Burland

Faith at Home

Faith Focus

- The Mass is a meal of thanksgiving.

- Jesus is the Bread of Life.

- In Holy Communion we are united to Jesus and the Church. We share in the promise of life forever with God.

Ritual Focus
Sharing a Meal

The celebration focused on sharing a meal. You prayed a blessing prayer and shared food. During the week, use the Blessing Prayer on page 149 as the prayer before your main meal.

Family Prayer

Lord, thank you for all the gifts you have given us. Thank you for family and friends. Help us grow strong in love for one another and for you. Send us the Holy Spirit to show us how to share your life and love with others. Amen.

Act

Share Together Plan a special meal of remembering and celebration with your family members. Decide whether it will be at home or at a restaurant. If it is at home, share in the preparation of the food. Ask each family member to bring pictures, symbols, or souvenirs of their favorite time as a family. Share the memories during the meal, and pray the blessings on page 149 before and after your meal.

Do Together As a family, prepare a meal for an elderly couple, or a family in which a parent is sick or a new baby has arrived. Plan the meal, contact the family to choose a convenient time, prepare the meal, and deliver it. As an alternative, volunteer to serve meals at a soup kitchen or Catholic Worker house.

 www.harcourtreligion.com
Visit our Web site for weekly scripture readings and questions, family resources, and more activities.

14 We Go Forth

We Gather

Procession

As you sing, walk forward slowly. Follow the person carrying the Bible.

🎼 *Sing together.*

Go now, love each other.
Thanks be to God.
We will be your spirit.
We will be your peace.
Let us love each other.
Lead us to the feast.

© 1998, Tom Kendzia and Gary Daigle,
Published by OCP Publications

Leader: Let us pray.

Make the Sign of the Cross together.

We Listen

Leader: Loving God, open our hearts to the Holy Spirit as we listen to your word. We ask this through Jesus Christ our Lord.

All: Amen.

Leader: A reading from the Acts of the Apostles.

Read Acts 2:1–41.

The word of the Lord.

All: Thanks be to God.

Sit silently.

Ritual Focus: Blessing for a Mission

Come forward and gather around the holy water.

Sprinkle candidates with water.

Leader: Just as the disciples were filled with the Holy Spirit and told the good news in word and action, so are we. Let us pray for God's blessing.

Lord, you came on earth to serve others. May your example strengthen us.

All: Amen.

Leader: Through your dying and rising, you made a new world where we are all neighbors called to love one another. May we live our lives according to your Gospel.

All: Amen.

Leader: Let us pray that God, who is love, will light our hearts with the fire of the Holy Spirit and give us a love for others.

Bow your heads and pray for God's blessing.

Blessed are you God of mercy. Through your Son, Jesus, you gave us an example of love.

Send down your blessing on these your children. Help them to generously serve others when they see their need. Let them serve you in their neighbor.

All: Amen.

ADAPTED FROM THE BOOK OF BLESSIGNS, 587

We Go Forth

Make the Sign of the Cross with the water.

Leader: Go forth now to love and serve the Lord.

All: Thanks be to God.

 Sing the opening song together.

Being Blessed

SIGNS OF FAITH

Blessing

A blessing is an action using words and gestures to ask God to show his kindness to us. There are many kinds of blessings. The Church blesses people and objects. Parents are blessed when their children are baptized. Animals are blessed on the feast of Saint Francis. Parents bless children at night or when they wake in the morning. The priest blesses special objects such as rosaries. At Mass the priest blesses the assembly.

Reflect

Blessing for a mission Think and write about the celebration. Go back and read the Blessing Prayer on page 159. Then write a few sentences to complete the journal entries below.

Today I was blessed. I felt really

_____

_____

_____

_____

I am being blessed to go out and serve others. I think that means

_____

_____

_____

_____

Sent on Mission

Have you ever been sent to do a special job? Being sent means you are trusted. You represent someone else. You are responsible. Someone is counting on you. Without you, the job will not get done.

At the end of Mass, we are sent to carry the message of God's love to others. We are sent to help carry out the work of Jesus in the world. The word *Mass* comes from a word that means "to be sent on a mission." Receiving Jesus in Holy Communion strengthens us to love and serve others. We go out from Mass with God's blessing.

SIGNS OF FAITH

Witness

At the end of Mass, we are sent forth to be witnesses of faith in Jesus' presence in the world today. A witness is somebody who sees or hears something and tells others about it. We are witnesses to Jesus' presence when we tell others about him in our words and in our actions.

The Holy Spirit

Faith Focus

What happens when we receive the Holy Spirit?

Before Jesus returned to his Father in heaven, he gave his disciples a mission. He wanted them to teach others about his message. Jesus promised the disciples he would send the Holy Spirit to help them with their mission. Fifty days after Jesus' Resurrection, his promise came true.

Scripture

ACTS 2:1–41

Pentecost

During the feast of Pentecost, the disciples were all in one place together. Suddenly, there came from the sky a noise like a strong driving wind, and it filled the entire house in which they were sitting. Then there appeared tongues as of fire, which parted and came to rest on each one of them. And they were all filled with the Holy Spirit and began to speak in different languages.

They went out into the street and began to tell the crowd about Jesus and his message. The people who listened were surprised because the disciples were speaking in different languages. They wondered what had happened.

Peter raised his voice and said, "What has happened is the work of the Holy Spirit. Jesus of Nazareth has sent the Holy Spirit as he promised." Then Peter said, "This Jesus whom you crucified has been raised from the dead. He is the Messiah." When the people heard this they asked Peter and the other Apostles, "What are we to do my brothers?" Peter told them, "Repent and be baptized, every one of you, in the name of Jesus Christ for the forgiveness of your sins; and you will receive the gift of the holy Spirit." Those who accepted his message were baptized, and about three thousand persons were added that day.

BASED ON ACTS 2:1–41

❓ **What did the Holy Spirit do for the disciples?**

❓ **How does the Holy Spirit help you?**

Faith at Home

Read the scripture story with your family members. Discuss everyone's responses to the questions. Ask family members to share times when they called on the Holy Spirit for help. Review the prayer Come, Holy Spirit on page 191. Choose an appropriate time each day to pray the prayer.

Share

Write a poem   On a separate sheet of paper, create your own poem about the Holy Spirit. Use at least five of the words below.

Holy Spirit	wind	wide	gift
in	be	guide	soar
today	pray	fire	fill

We Are Sent

SIGNS OF FAITH

Deacon

A **deacon** is a man ordained by the bishop to do works of charity and to have a special role in worship. Some deacons become priests. Other deacons do not, but they help the bishop and care for people who need it. All deacons can baptize and witness a marriage. At Mass deacons may carry the Book of the Gospels, read the Gospel, and preach. They can also send us forth for mission at the end of Mass.

Faith Focus

How do we love and serve Jesus?

Like Peter and the disciples, Jesus promises us the Holy Spirit. The Holy Spirit is with us always. The Holy Spirit helps us:

- tell others about his love
- do the work of a disciple
- forgive others
- care about people who need help, especially those who are poor

164

Go Forth

At the end of Mass, we are sent forth to serve others. The priest or deacon says, "Go in peace to love and serve the Lord." We respond, "Thanks be to God." We go forth to share the joyful good news that Jesus is alive. We share the good news by what we say and what we do.

When we leave the church after Mass, we are different from when we came in. Participating in the Eucharist changes us. It brings us closer to God the Father, Son, and Holy Spirit. It also brings us closer to one another. Just as many grains of wheat make one loaf of bread, in the Eucharist we become one body. We are filled with God's grace and love. We go forth to serve others. We go forth to help those who need our help. We love and serve Jesus when we love and serve one another.

? **How will you ask the Holy Spirit to help you look at your life?**

Faith at Home

Discuss your response to the question with your family members. Talk about ways in which you can serve others within your family. Suggest that every family member decide to serve another member without that person knowing it.

Sent to Serve

Respond

Draw a slide presentation In the frames provided, draw a slide presentation that shows how you will live out your mission as part of the Body of Christ.

Closing Blessing

Gather and begin with the Sign of the Cross.

Leader: God, our Father, send us forth to tell the world about your love.

All: Amen.

Leader: Jesus, our Savior, send us forth to serve others.

All: Amen.

Leader: Holy Spirit, guide us to see the places where we are called to love and serve.

All: Amen.

 Sing together.

Go now, love each other.
Thanks be to God.
We will be your spirit.
We will be your peace.
Let us love each other.
Lead us to the feast.

Faith at Home

Faith Focus

- The Eucharist changes us.

- The Holy Spirit helps us to live out our mission.

- At Mass we are sent forth to love and serve others.

Ritual Focus
Blessing for Mission

The celebration focused on being sent forth for mission. You were blessed by your catechist and sent forth. Talk with family members about doing a family ritual of blessing each other with the Sign of the Cross on the forehead when you leave the house in the morning or at other times you decide would be appropriate.

Family Prayer

Come Holy Spirit, show us the way and give us the strength to love and serve others. Amen.

Act

Share Together Make a list of ways members of your family show love and care for each other. Then brainstorm together other ways the family might continue to show love and care. Suggest a family "love and serve" week. Write the names of family members on a slip of paper. Have each member draw a name. Invite family members to do some "love and serve" actions for that person.

Do Together Obtain copies of the parish bulletin or newsletter. With your family, go through it and locate parish activities of service and outreach. Choose one that the whole family can get involved in, and call the parish to volunteer. After volunteering, hold a family discussion about the experience and how it felt to love and serve others.

Love and Serve Week

GO **ONLINE** www.harcourtreligion.com
Visit our Web site for weekly scripture readings and questions, family resources, and more activities.

Catholic Source Book

Words of Faith

altar The table of the Eucharist. The Liturgy of the Eucharist is celebrated at the altar.

altar server A person who helps the priest and deacon at Mass.

ambo The reading stand from which the Scriptures are proclaimed. It is sometimes called the lectern.

assembly The baptized community gathered to celebrate the Eucharist, the sacraments, or other liturgy.

Baptism One of the three Sacraments of Initiation. Baptism gives us new life in God and makes us members of the Church.

baptismal font A bowl-shaped container or pool of water used for Baptism. The word *font* means "fountain."

Bible God's word written in human words. The Bible is the holy book of the Church.

Blessed Sacrament Another name for the Body and Blood of Jesus.

blessing An action using words and gestures which asks God to show his kindness to us.

Body of Christ A name for the Church. It tells us that Christ is the head and the baptized are the members of the body.

Book of the Gospels A decorated book containing the readings from the four Gospels used during the Liturgy of the Word.

cantor The leader of song during the Mass and other Church celebrations.

chalice The special silver or gold cup used at Mass to hold the wine that becomes the Blood of Christ.

chrism The oil blessed by the bishop used in the Sacraments of Baptism, Confirmation, and Holy Orders.

Christian The name given to people who are baptized and follow Jesus.

Church The community of all baptized people who believe in God and follow Jesus.

ciborium The special silver or gold container used at Mass to hold the smaller consecrated Hosts for communion. A covered ciborium also holds the Blessed Sacrament in the tabernacle.

collection The gifts of money collected from members of the assembly and presented during the time of the Preparation of the Altar.

Confirmation One of the three Sacraments of Initiation. It is the sacrament that strengthens the life of God we received at Baptism and seals us with the gift of the Holy Spirit.

Confiteor A prayer of sorrow for sin. In it each person tells God and the Church family, "I am sorry." We ask for forgiveness.

consecration The part of the Eucharistic Prayer when, through the prayers and actions of the priest and the power of the Holy Spirit, the gifts of bread and wine become the Body and Blood of Jesus.

cruets Small pitchers or containers that hold the water and wine used at Mass.

deacon A man who is ordained to serve the Church. Deacons may baptize, proclaim the Gospel, preach, assist the priest at Mass, witness marriages, and do works of charity.

Eucharist One of the three Sacraments of Initiation. It is the sacrament of the Body and Blood of Christ. Jesus is truly and really present in the Eucharist. The word *Eucharist* means "thanksgiving."

grace A sharing in God's own life.

Holy Communion The Body and Blood of Christ that we receive in the Eucharist.

Holy Trinity The three Persons in one God: God the Father, God the Son, and God the Holy Spirit.

host A round piece of unleavened bread used at Mass. When the host is consecrated at Mass, it becomes the Body and Blood of Christ.

incense Oils and spices that are burned in liturgical celebrations to show honor for holy things. It is also used as a sign of our prayers rising to God.

Lamb of God   A title for Jesus that reminds us that he offered his life through suffering and death to take away our sins.

 lectionary   The book of scripture readings used at Mass.

lector   A person who proclaims God's word at Mass or other liturgical celebrations. The word *lector* means "reader."

Liturgy of the Eucharist   The second main part of the Mass. It is the time when we call on the Holy Spirit and the priest consecrates the bread and wine. We remember and give thanks for all of God's gifts, especially Jesus' life, death, and Resurrection.

Liturgy of the Word   The first main part of the Mass. It is the time when we listen to God's word in the Scriptures.

Mass   Another name for the Eucharist.

memorial   Another word for remembering. In the Mass, it means to remember and proclaim God's works.

mission   A job or duty someone is sent to do and takes responsibility for. The Church's mission is to announce the good news of God's kingdom.

mystery   Something we believe about God and his actions, but we do not understand how it happens.

original sin   The first sin committed by the first humans.

Paschal candle Another name for the Easter Candle that is lit at the Easter Vigil.

paten The silver or gold plate or dish used at Mass to hold the large host.

Pentecost The feast that celebrates the coming of the Holy Spirit on the Apostles and disciples fifty days after Easter. We celebrate this day as the beginning of the Church.

People of God A name for the Church which tells us that we are sent by Christ to preach God's love to all people.

prayer Talking and listening to God. It is raising our minds and hearts to God.

preparation of the altar and gifts The part of the Mass when the altar is prepared and members of the assembly bring the bread and wine, which will become the Body and Blood of Jesus, to the priest at the altar.

priest A man who is ordained to serve God and lead the Church by celebrating the sacraments, preaching and presiding at Mass, and performing other spiritual works.

procession A group of people moving forward as part of a celebration.

sacrament A holy sign that comes from Jesus, which gives us a share in God's life.

sacramentary The book containing the Order of the Mass, special celebrations during the year, and various prayers used by the priest at Mass.

Sacraments of Initiation The three Sacraments of Baptism, Confirmation, and Holy Eucharist that together make us full members of the Church. They are signs that we belong to God and to the Catholic Church.

sanctuary The part of the church where the altar and ambo are located. The word *sanctuary* means "holy place."

Sign of Peace The sign of peace is an action prayer that we exchange before Communion as a sign to wish God's peace on those who receive it. It shows that we are one in Christ's love.

tabernacle The container in which the Blessed Sacrament is kept. It may be located in the sanctuary or a special chapel in the church. A lamp or candle is kept burning near the tabernacle as a sign that Jesus is present. The word *tabernacle* means "meeting place."

unity A word that means to be one with others.

usher A person of hospitality who welcomes members of the assembly to Mass and helps direct processions and collections.

vestments The special clothing worn by the priest and some others for Mass and other liturgical celebrations.

Order of the Mass

Every Sunday we gather together united as one with all the members of the Church to give praise and thanks to God.

Introductory Rites

During the Introductory Rites, we prepare to listen to God's word and prepare to celebrate the Eucharist.

Entrance

The priest, deacon, and other ministers begin the procession to the altar. We stand and sing. The Greeting and our response shows that we are gathered together as the Church.

Greeting of the Altar and the People

When the procession reaches the altar, the priest, deacon, and other ministers make a profound bow. The priest and deacon also kiss the altar as a sign of reverence. At special times the priest will burn incense at the cross and altar. The priest goes to his chair and leads us in the Sign of the Cross and Greeting.

Priest: In the name of the Father, and of the Son, and of the Holy Spirit.

People: Amen.

Priest: The grace and peace of God our Father and the Lord Jesus Christ be with you.

People: And also with you.

Rite of Sprinkling with Holy Water

On some Sundays, the priest does a Rite of Sprinkling in place of the Penitential Rite. We are blessed with holy water to remind us of our Baptism.

Penitential Rite

The priest invites the assembly to confess our sins together.

Confiteor

I confess to Almighty God
and to you, my brothers and sisters,
that I have sinned through my own fault,
in my thoughts and in my words,
in what I have done,
and in what I have failed to do;
and I ask Blessed Mary ever virgin,
all the angels and saints,
and you, my brothers and sisters,
to pray for me to the Lord our God.

Lord Have Mercy

Priest: Lord, have mercy.

People: Lord, have mercy.

Priest: Christ, have mercy.

People: Christ, have mercy.

Priest: Lord, have mercy.

People: Lord, have mercy.

Priest: May almighty God have mercy on us, forgive us our sins, and bring us to everlasting life.

People: Amen.

Gloria

On some Sundays, we praise God the Father, the Son, and the Holy Spirit.

Glory to God in the highest,
and peace to his people on earth.
Lord God, heavenly King,
almighty God and Father,
we worship you, we give you thanks,
we praise you for your glory.
Lord Jesus Christ, only Son of the Father,
Lord God, Lamb of God,
you take away the sin of the world:
have mercy on us;
you are seated at the right hand of the
Father:
receive our prayer.
For you alone are the Holy One,
you alone are the Lord,
you alone are the Most High,
Jesus Christ,
with the Holy Spirit,
in the glory of God the Father. Amen.

Collect

The priest invites us to pray. We are silent for a moment and remember we are in God's presence. We think about what we want to pray for.

Priest: Let us pray…
People: Amen.

Liturgy of the Word

The Liturgy of the Word is celebrated at every Mass. We listen to God's word in the Readings and Homily, and we respond to God's word in the Creed and Prayers of the Faithful. The lectors and the priest or deacon read the readings from the ambo.

First Reading

We sit and listen to God's word from the Old Testament or the Acts of the Apostles. At the end of the reading, we respond:

Reader: The word of the Lord.
People: Thanks be to God.

Responsorial Psalm

At the end of the first reading, the cantor, or song leader, leads us in singing a psalm from the Old Testament.

People: Sing or say the refrain.

Second Reading

We listen to God's word from the New Testament books that are not Gospels. At the end of the reading, we respond:

Reader: The word of the Lord.
People: Thanks be to God.

Acclamation Before the Gospel

We stand and welcome the Lord, who speaks to us in the Gospel reading. We sing an Alleluia or another acclamation to profess our faith in God's presence.

People: Sing or say the Alleluia or Gospel Acclamation.

Gospel

Priest or deacon: The Lord be with you.

People: And also with you.

Priest or deacon: A reading from the holy Gospel according to…

People: Glory to you, Lord.

The priest and people make the Sign of the Cross on the forehead, lips, and heart.

At the end of the Gospel, we respond:

Priest or deacon: The Gospel of the Lord.

People: Praise to you, Lord Jesus Christ.

Homily

We sit and listen. The priest or deacon helps us understand the word of God. He shows us how we can live as Jesus' disciples.

Profession of Faith

We stand and respond to the readings by saying the Creed. We profess our faith in God the Father, God the Son, and God the Holy Spirit. We pray the Nicene Creed or the Apostles' Creed.

(For Nicene Creed, see page 178. For Apostles' Creed, see page 188.)

Nicene Creed

People:

We believe in one God,
   the Father, the Almighty,
   maker of heaven and earth,
   of all that is seen and unseen.
We believe in one Lord, Jesus Christ,
   the only Son of God,
   eternally begotten of the Father,
   God from God, Light from Light,
   true God from true God,
   begotten, not made, one in Being
      with the Father.
   Through him all things were made.
   For us men and for our salvation
      he came down from heaven:
   by the power of the Holy Spirit
      he was born of the Virgin Mary,
         and became man.
   For our sake he was crucified under
      Pontius Pilate;
   he suffered, died, and was buried.

On the third day he rose again
   in fulfillment of the Scriptures;
   he ascended into heaven
      and is seated at the right hand of
         the Father.
He will come again in glory
   to judge the living and the dead,
   and his kingdom will have no end.
We believe in the Holy Spirit, the
   Lord, the giver of life,
   who proceeds from the Father
      and the Son.
   With the Father and the Son he is
      worshiped and glorified.
   He has spoken through the
      Prophets.
We believe in one holy
   catholic and apostolic Church.
We acknowledge one baptism for
   the forgiveness of sins.
We look for the resurrection of
   the dead, and the life of the world
      to come. Amen.

General Intercessions

We stand and the priest, deacon, or a layperson leads us in praying for the needs of the Church, the world, those who need our prayers, and our local community. We say or sing the response that the leader tells us to say or sing.

Liturgy of the Eucharist

During the Liturgy of the Eucharist, we bring our gifts of bread and wine to the altar. We give thanks to God the Father for all the ways he has saved us. Our gifts of bread and wine become the Body and Blood of Christ. We all receive the Lord's Body and the Lord's Blood in communion.

Preparation of the Gifts

We sit as the gifts of bread and wine are brought to the altar. The altar is prepared as the collection is taken up. Sometimes we sing a song during the preparation.

The priest lifts up the bread and prays:

Priest: Blessed are you, Lord God of all creation.
Through your goodness we have this bread to offer which earth has given and human hands have made. It will become for us the bread of life.

People: Blessed be God forever.

The priest lifts up the chalice of wine and prays:

Priest: Blessed are you, Lord God of all creation.
Through your goodness we have this wine to offer, fruit of the vine and work of human hands.
It will become our spiritual drink.

People: Blessed be God forever.

The priest calls us to pray.

Priest: Pray, my brothers and sisters, that our sacrifice may be acceptable to God, the almighty Father.

People: May the Lord accept the sacrifice at your hands
for the praise and glory of his name,
for our good,
and the good of all his Church.

Prayer over the Offerings

We stand and pray with the priest. We prepare for the Eucharistic Prayer.

People: Amen.

Eucharistic Prayer

This is the central prayer of the Eucharist. It is a prayer of thanksgiving and making holy.

Preface

The priest invites us to pray. We say or sing the preface.

Priest: The Lord be with you.

People: And also with you.

Priest: Lift up your hearts.

People: We lift them up to the Lord.

Priest: Let us give thanks to the Lord our God.

People: It is right to give him thanks and praise.

Acclamation

Together with the priest, we say or sing:

Holy, holy, holy Lord, God of power
  and might,
Heaven and earth are full of your glory.
Hosanna in the Highest.
Blessed is he who comes in the name
  of the Lord.
Hosanna in the highest.

The priest continues to pray the Eucharistic prayer. During the Eucharistic prayer the priest tells the story of all of God's saving actions.

Consecration

The priest takes the bread and says the words of Jesus:

Take this, all of you, and eat it:
this is my Body which will be given up
  for you.

The priest holds up the consecrated bread, the Host, which is now the Body of Christ.

Then the priest takes the chalice, the cup of wine, and says the words of Jesus:

> Take this, all of you, and drink from it:
> this is the cup of my Blood,
> the Blood of the new and everlasting covenant.
> It will be shed for you and for all
> so that sins may be forgiven.
> Do this in memory of me.

The bread and wine become the Body and Blood of Jesus through the power of the Holy Spirit and the words and actions of the priest. Jesus is truly present under the appearances of bread and wine. We proclaim our faith in Jesus.

Memorial Acclamation

Priest or deacon: Let us proclaim the mystery of faith.

People: Christ has died,
Christ is risen,
Christ will come again.

The priest continues the Eucharistic Prayer. He prays for the whole Church, those who are living and those who are dead. He ends the prayer by singing or saying aloud:

Priest: Through him, with him, in him, in the unity of the Holy Spirit, all glory and honor is yours, almighty Father, for ever and ever.

People: Amen.

Communion Rite

We stand for the Lord's Prayer. We pray for our daily bread. We pray our sins will be forgiven.

Lord's Prayer

People: Our Father, who art in heaven,
hallowed be thy name;
thy kingdom come;
thy will be done on earth as it is
in heaven.
Give us this day our daily bread;
and forgive us our trespasses
as we forgive those who trespass
against us;
and lead us not into temptation,
But deliver us from evil.

Priest: Deliver us, Lord, from every
evil…

People: For the kingdom, the power
and the glory are yours,
now and forever.

Sign of Peace

The priest or deacon invites us to share a Sign of Peace with those around us. We pray for peace and that the Church and the world will be united as one.

Priest: The peace of the Lord be with
you always.

People: And also with you.

We offer one another a sign of peace.

Breaking of the Bread

Just as Jesus broke bread at the Last Supper and gave it to his disciples, the priest breaks the consecrated bread and puts a piece of it into the chalice to show the unity of Jesus' Body and Blood. During the breaking of the bread, we say or sing:

People: Lamb of God, you take away the sins of the world: have mercy on us.
Lamb of God, you take away the sins of the world: have mercy on us.
Lamb of God, you take away the sins of the world: grant us peace.

Communion

The priest shows us the consecrated bread. He holds the Host up and invites us to the banquet of the Lord. We respond:

People: Lord, I am not worthy to receive you, but only say the word and I shall be healed.

The priest receives Holy Communion. We sing the Communion hymn. When it is time, we walk in procession to receive Holy Communion. The minister offers us the consecrated bread, the Body of Christ. We bow our heads as a sign of reverence before receiving the Body of Christ.

Priest or extraordinary minister: The Body of Christ.
People: Amen.

We receive the Body of Christ in our hand or on our tongue. We reverently chew and swallow the consecrated bread.

If we are receiving the consecrated wine, the Blood of Christ, the minister offers us the cup. We bow our head as a sign of reverence before receiving the Blood of Christ.

Priest or extraordinary minister: The Blood of Christ.

People: Amen.

We return to our seats and give thanks for the wonderful gift of Jesus we have received in Communion.

When the distribution of Communion is finished, the priest and people pray privately. A song may be sung at this time.

Prayer After Communion

We stand. The priest invites us to pray with him as he asks God to help us live as God's People, the Body of Christ.

Priest: Let us pray…

People: Amen.

Concluding Rite

We stand for the concluding rite. The priest greets us, blesses us in the name of the Holy Trinity, and sends us forth to live as Jesus' disciples.

Greeting

Priest: The Lord be with you.

People: And also with you.

Blessing

Priest: May Almighty God bless you in the name of the Father, the Son, and the Holy Spirit.

People: Amen.

Dismissal

Priest: Go in peace to love and serve the Lord.

People: Thanks be to God.

We sing a hymn of praise. The priest kisses the altar as a sign of reverence. He and the other ministers leave in procession.

Holy Communion

Rules for Receiving Holy Communion

- Only baptized Catholics may receive Communion.

- To receive Holy Communion, we must be in the state of grace, free from mortal sin. If we have sinned mortally, we must first go to the Sacrament of Reconciliation and receive absolution before receiving Holy Communion. When we are sorry for our venial sins, receiving Holy Communion frees us from them.

- To honor the Lord, we fast for one hour before the time we receive Communion. This means we go without food or drink, except water or medicine.

- Catholics are required to receive Holy Communion at least once a year during Easter time. But we are encouraged to receive Communion every time we participate in the Mass.

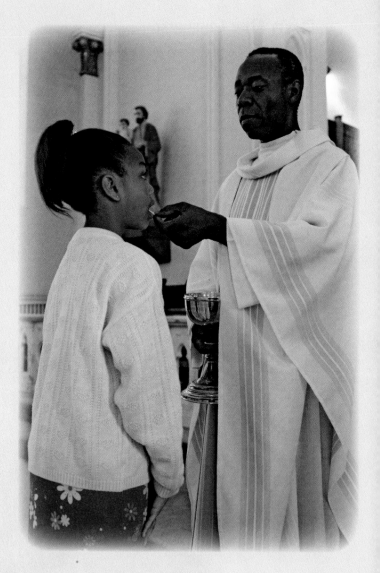

How to Receive Communion

When we receive Jesus in Holy Communion, we welcome him by showing reverence. These steps can help you.

- Fold your hands, and join in the singing as you wait in line.

- When it is your turn, you can receive the Body of Christ in your hand or on your tongue.

- When you are shown the Eucharist, bow in reverence.

- To receive the Body of Christ in your hand, hold your hands out with the palms up. Place one hand underneath the other, and cup your hands slightly.

- To receive the Host on your tongue, fold your hands, open your mouth, and put your tongue out.

- The person who offers you Communion will say, "The Body of Christ." You say, "Amen." The priest, deacon, or extraordinary minister of Holy Communion places the Host in your hand or on your tongue. Step aside, and chew and swallow the host.

- You may choose to drink from the cup. When the cup is offered to you, the person will say, "The Blood of Christ." You say, "Amen." Take a small sip.

- Return to your place in church. Pray quietly in your own words. Thank Jesus for being with you.

Catholic Prayers

Lord's Prayer

Our Father, who art in heaven,
hallowed be thy name;
thy kingdom come;
thy will be done on earth as it is
  in heaven.
Give us this day our daily bread;
and forgive us our trespasses
as we forgive those who trespass
  against us;
and lead us not into temptation,
but deliver us from evil.
Amen.

Apostles' Creed

I believe in God, the Father almighty,
  creator of heaven and earth.
I believe in Jesus Christ, his only Son,
  our Lord.
    He was conceived by the power of
      the Holy Spirit
    and born of the Virgin Mary.
    He suffered under Pontius Pilate,
    was crucified, died, and was buried.
    He descended to the dead.
    On the third day, he rose again.
    He ascended into heaven,
      and is seated at the right hand of the
        Father.
    He will come again to judge the living
      and the dead.
I believe in the Holy Spirit,
    the holy catholic Church,
    the communion of saints,
    the forgiveness of sins,
    the resurrection of the body,
    and the life everlasting.
Amen.

Nicene Creed

We believe in one God,
   the Father, the Almighty,
   maker of heaven and earth,
   of all that is seen and unseen.
We believe in one Lord, Jesus Christ,
   the only Son of God,
   eternally begotten of the Father,
God from God, Light from Light,
true God from true God,
begotten, not made, one in Being
      with the Father.
   Through him all things were made.
   For us men and for our salvation
      he came down from heaven:
by the power of the Holy Spirit
   he was born of the Virgin Mary,
      and became man.
For our sake he was crucified under
      Pontius Pilate;
he suffered, died, and was buried.
On the third day he rose again
   in fulfillment of the Scriptures;
   he ascended into heaven
      and is seated at the right hand of
      the Father.

He will come again in glory
   to judge the living and the dead,
   and his kingdom will have
      no end.
We believe in the Holy Spirit, the
   Lord, the giver of life,
who proceeds from the Father and
   the Son.
With the Father and the Son he is
   worshiped and glorified.
He has spoken through the
   Prophets.
We believe in one holy catholic and
   apostolic Church.
We acknowledge one baptism for
   the forgiveness of sins.
We look for the resurrection of the
   dead, and the life of the world to
   come. Amen.

Confiteor

I confess to Almighty God
and to you, my brothers and sisters,
that I have sinned through my own fault,
in my thoughts and in my words,
in what I have done,
and in what I have failed to do;
and I ask Blessed Mary ever virgin,
all the angels and saints,
and you, my brothers and sisters,
to pray for me to the Lord our God.

Gloria

Glory to God in the highest,
and peace to his people on earth.
Lord God, heavenly King,
almighty God and Father,
we worship you, we give you thanks,
we praise you for your glory.
Lord Jesus Christ, only Son of the Father,
Lord God, Lamb of God,
you take away the sin of the world:
have mercy on us;
you are seated at the right hand of the
Father:
receive our prayer.
For you alone are the Holy One,
you alone are the Lord,
you alone are the Most High,
Jesus Christ,
with the Holy Spirit,
in the glory of God the Father.
Amen.

Hail Mary

Hail, Mary, full of grace!
The Lord is with you!
Blessed are you among women,
and blessed is the fruit of your
    womb, Jesus.
Holy Mary, Mother of God,
pray for us sinners,
now and at the hour of our death.
Amen.

Come, Holy Spirit

Come, Holy Spirit, fill the hearts of your
    faithful
And kindle in them the fire of your love.
Send forth your Spirit and they shall be
    created.
And you shall renew the face of the
    earth.

Grace Before Meals

Bless us, O Lord, and these your gifts,
which we are about to receive
from your goodness.
Through Christ our Lord.
Amen.

Grace After Meals

We give you thanks for all your gifts,
almighty God,
living and reigning now and forever.
Amen.

Boldfaced numbers refer to pages on which the terms are defined in the *Candidate's Book*.